**Turning Girls into Ladi...**
**A Multicultural Behavioral A...**

Youth Workbook

Lessons 1-15

By Dr. James Parker Griffin, Jr., L.P.C., C.A.M.S. II

Copyright 2020

EyeOpening Media Productions, LLC, Publisher

## DEDICATION

This workbook is dedicated to Brehana, Amber, and Dee, each of whom

provided an irreplaceable source of inspiration in the development of the program.

**Turning Girls into Ladies**
**A Multicultural Behavioral Approach**

*Lesson Topics*

1. INTRODUCTION TO WOMANHOOD
2. PREPARING GIRLS TO BE LADIES WHO LEAD
3. SUPPORTING YOUR PEERS
4. HEALTH AND FITNESS
5. FEMALE-MALE RELATIONSHIPS
6. RESPECT FOR MEN--PART 1
7. RESPECT FOR MEN--PART 2
8. MOTHERHOOD
9. WOMANHOOD AND MASS MEDIA:
   MAKING SENSE OF MUSIC, TELEVISION, AND PRINT
10. HOW TO HANDLE PEOPLE WHO TREAT YOU UNFAIRLY
11. HOW TO DEAL WITH AUTHORITIES
12. LEARNING TO PREVENT VIOLENCE, MANAGE CONFLICT, AND SELECT
    REAL FRIENDS
13. SPIRITUALITY
14. FAST MONEY VS. HONEST MONEY: BECOMING A SUCCESS
15. BECOMING A MATURE, WELL-ROUNDED LADY

This guide is designed to help young females to increase awareness and gain skills to develop into mature ladies in their personal, family, and community relationships.

The activities in this guide will help you to acquire:

- Leadership skills

- Relationship building skills
    —Sister to sister
    —Female to male
- A clear idea of who you are
- Promote responsible self-love
- New ways of thinking
- Ways to stay out of trouble
- Accelerated pathways to success
- Responsibility in family and community
- Promote consideration for other people

To obtain the maximum benefits of this guide, you need to remain actively involved during each exercise. The guide will help you reach success if you use it.

An important aim of this program is to encourage teenage and young adult females to become leaders. This can take place on different levels. These include acting like a girl with no leadership or showing leadership on the individual, boss, community, or national levels. This training focuses on helping you move to the adult level of leadership. Let's look at what these levels can look like.

| LEADERSHIP TYPE & AN EXAMPLE OF A PERSON(S) IN EACH GROUP | Important Actions by Leadership Level |
|---|---|
| Complete countries or the whole world SOCIETAL LEADERSHIP IV. The President | Champions a cause, promotes a beneficial mission for others in society. |
| Community and organizations GROUP LEADERSHIP III. Chief executive officer for a company, Small business owner, Faith leader for a congregation, etc. | Supervises people manage projects administers programs runs companies or organizations |
| LADIES' INDIVIDUAL LEADERSHIP It begins with you! II. MOST WORKING, SUPPORTIVE, ADULT FEMALES | Working toward standards for behaving like a confident lady: Responsible for resisting negative peer and media influences, thinks for herself, provides for herself and others; committed to promoting beneficial conditions for children, friends, family, and community. |
| GIRLHOOD I. | Lacking in responsible actions regarding herself and others; unaware of ways to behave like a mature person; depends on others instead of herself. |

# Turning Girls into Ladies

## A Multicultural, Behavioral Approach

## Lesson 1

# Turning Girls into Ladies

## A Multicultural, Behavioral Approach

## Lesson 1

**Introduction to the Development of Ladies**

**Learning Objectives**

You should learn what:

- Characteristics define ladyhood?
- Cultural points of view help shape your personal values regarding ladyhood?
- Behaviors distinguish girls from ladies?

**Exercise 1.1**
**What is LADYHOOD?**

**STEPS:** *What you do*

Take 5 minutes to think about the ways that you see what the word womanhood or ladyhood (becoming a polished, distinguished lady) means to you.

| LADYHOOD QUALITIES LIST 5 THINGS THAT SHOW THE DIFFERENCE BETWEEN A GIRL AND A LADY. | |
| --- | --- |
| 1. A girl is | a lady is |
| 2. A girl is | a lady is |
| 3. A girl is | a lady is |
| 4. A girl is | a lady is |
| 5. A girl is | a lady is |

**Exercise 1.2**
**Ladies: MOVING TOWARD SUCCESS**

Girlhood to Ladyhood

Future Female Leader
Your Road to Success

AN IMPORTANT PART of the WAY A mature female ACTS is that she plans her life in a direction that moves toward being financially responsible. She recognizes that if she does not look out for her success, there is no guarantee that anyone else will. This involves taking an active role in mastering the skills that lead to success. She avoids THINKING NEGATIVELY ABOUT other people (from other countries, for example) who make great sacrifices to become successful THEMSELVES. Instead, the mature LADY tries to learn from the successes of other people around her. She imitates success and combines imitation with high motivation in order to excel.

Instead of complaining about the great opportunities that others have, she searches for or creates her own opportunities. She recognizes that part of success is a series of short-term setbacks. THEREFORE, she never gives up on a goal and looks for ways to RISE ABOVE setbacks when they occur. She views these setbacks as temporary obstacles that she will overcome eventually if she never stops trying.

The mature LADY looks AT PEOPLE AND SITUATIONS around her and anticipates which opportunities exist for self-improvement and for increasing her wealth and health. This includes working hard to become as healthy as she can both physically and mentally. More information on this subject appears in some of the later lessons in the training.

Of course, money is not everything when it comes to being a successful mature leader. Understand that there are more important things in life than money alone. Some of them include developing self-respect, respect for others, integrity, character, and decency. Taking the initiative to cultivate these qualities within yourself is an important part of being a whole lady. The key to planning your life is to become a self-starter and to create balance in your life so that no SINGLE part of your life overshadows any other part.

Although it is very important to work to generate income, it is not the only way to express your ability as a self-starter. BEING A SELF-STARTER is an important skill that cuts across many areas. For example, the mature female leader must be responsible for actively organizing and maintaining her living quarters, family matters, and work responsibilities, to name a few. In the future, more than ever before, LADIES WHO ARE LEADERS will need to be self-starters to compete in world-wide BUSINESSES that are developing across the globe. MOTIVATING YOURSELF AND LEARNING HOW TO GET ALONG WITH PEOPLE DIFFERENT FROM YOU will be ABSOLUTELY

NECESSARY TO ACHIEVE SUCCESS IN THE FUTURE regardless of a person's race, ethnic background or religious beliefs.

**Exercise 1.3**
**Responsible Lady: DEFINING What They Do**

STEPS: What you do

Study the following definition: What is a mature lady?

Working definition:

MATURE Lady

As early as twelve years old, a truly mature lady acts responsibly toward her friends, family, community, men, and children by acting in ways to please them. Females who hit men or take advantage of them sexually are not real ladies. Real ladies only tear down parts of the community when it is necessary to build something new, like a shopping center or housing development. Real ladies work to make people, places, and things better than they were when they first came into contact with them. This is what tells you that a female is a mature lady and a true leader.

STEPS: What you do

Read the stories on the next page, then use the Mature or Less Mature Table (1) to identify the matching ladyhood traits.

Story A

Trisha is a 21-year-old female who lived on the southeast side of a large urban city. She has been dating Andrew for three years. They have had talks about getting married, but there are problems that stem from some of Trisha's actions. Andrew recently went to the department store to purchase some new shoes. He discovered that his $8,000 credit card limit had been maxed out. In other words, Andrew used up all of the available credit to make purchases on the credit card. This incident occurred a week after learning that Trisha had made $700 worth of new purchases on the cell phone account. Trisha has been using Andrew's car and returned it with the gas needle on empty. Once, she offered to make up for running the gas out of the car by giving him a $5.00 bill. When Andrew demanded that Trisha pay for his bills, she slapped him, knocking him against the wall. She then laughed at him and said, "You fool. I'm a grown woman, and I do what I want to do when I get ready to do it. If you don't like it, you can find some other pushover to hang out with." Andrew replied, "How dare you?" Trisha slapped him again and said, "How dare I what?" Andrew ran into the bathroom, locked the door behind him, and called the police. Trisha was arrested, spent two weeks in jail, and lost her job.

Use Table 1 to identify characteristics in Column A or Column B that describe Trisha.

Write them here:

_____

_____

_____

_____

_____

_____

_____

_____

Story B

A young woman named Danielle was riding the five o'clock subway on her way home from work. She noticed a lady who appeared to be about 65 years old board and stands in front of her. The older woman appeared to be dead tired. The train was full, and there was nowhere for the older lady to sit. In an act of kindness and consideration, Danielle gave the older lady her seat. Just then, Danielle's friends started to act very badly by talking loudly and cursing without any consideration for anyone around them. Danielle asked her friends to stop cursing as a matter of respect for the older lady. One of her friends said, "Danelle, you don't ever want to have any fun." At the same time, the friends complied with Danielle's request. Looking at the older lady, some nodded, and one said she was sorry for their behavior. The lady expressed her sincere appreciation to them and smiled. Danielle told the older lady, "A real lady doesn't have to curse in order to get her point across. I'm sorry, ma'am, that we didn't show more respect for you or ourselves."

Use Table 1 to identify traits in Column A or Column B that describe girls versus ladies.

## Story C

Michelle Payne consistently takes care of her two children, ages 2 and 4, while her boyfriend often goes to nightclubs with his friends. Michelle takes her children to the park to spend time with them, and to stores to buy them clothes. She enjoys laughing with the children and giving them hugs and kisses. Her friends see her as a softy. Some told her that it was not her job to be "taking care of the kids." "Let their dad do that stuff," they insisted. They went so far as to tell Michelle that she should not just have one boyfriend. "Date as many men as you can," they said. Michelle told her friends they were wrong and to "mind their own business." Instead of being persuaded, Michelle began to back away from her girlfriends from high school. Michelle made a point to hang out with her girlfriends less and less.

## Story D

Two sisters were running late to board a plane. It would have taken two hours to drive to the airport and park, so they decided to take the rail system. As they walked toward the rail system, three guys with guns stopped them. It was dark outside, and no one else was near. The situation caught them off guard. The three armed men surrounded them. One of the sisters said, "Whatever you guys want, you can have. We don't have any cash." Two of the men began to reach for the sisters' luggage. When they did this, the sisters started yelling for help and began to run in front of the approaching cars. One of the cars happened to be a police car. The policeman drove onto the sidewalk between the sisters. The officers had now drawn their guns, and one shouted, "Drop your weapons!" When one of the robbers refused to drop his weapon, one of the officers shot two of the criminals. One of the men died at the scene, and the other two were taken into custody.

Use Table 1 to identify characteristics in Column A or Column B that describe the sisters, and then describe the robbers.

| Ways to Describe Mature & Less Mature Females | |
| --- | --- |
| **TABLE 1** Ladyhood Development | |
| COLUMN A Ladies | COLUMN B Girls |
| 1. Takes responsibility for her actions. | 1. Usually acts as if she is more important than anyone else. |
| 2. Considers other people's feelings routinely. | 2. Easily influenced by peers. |
| 3. Promotes peaceful friendships. | 3. Corrupts people around her. |
| 4. Earns items that she uses personally. | 4. Reacts to bad experiences instead of preventing them from happening well before hand. |
| 5. Respects people. | 5. Physically mistreats men. |
| 6. Respects property. | 6. Thinks of herself more often than others. |
| 7. Obeys the law. | 7. Accepts bad ideas without considering the effects on others. |
| 8. Promotes healthy thoughts in people. | 8. Starts conflicts. |
| 9. Shows self-control. | 9. Uses other people's belongings without their permission. |
| 10. Maintains self-discipline. | 10. Takes advantage of guy's belongings. |
| 11. Makes people around her stronger. | 11. Shares little of herself with the community. |
| 12. Displays patience. | 12. Insists that self-control is pointless. |
| 13. Completes tasks without quitting. | 13. Jumps from project to project without finishing any one assignment. |
| 14. Tolerates others. | 14. Gets intoxicated often. |
| 15. Gives back to the community. | 15. Disrespects people. |
| 16. Refuses alcohol and other drugs. | 16. Wastes money. |

# Turning Girls into Ladies

## Preparing Girls to Be Ladies Who Lead

## Lesson 2

# Turning Girls into Ladies

## Preparing Girls to Be Ladies Who Lead

## Lesson 2

### Learning Objective

**You should learn:**
- **The behaviors distinguish girls from ladies**
- **To recognize different codes of conduct**

Exercise 2.1
Leadership from Women: RAP-PLEDGE WRITING EXERCISE

STEPS: What you do

Take 10 minutes to write a personal rap or pledge about becoming a female leader. Describe the ideal way you would like to see yourself 25 years from now. You can refer to Exercise 1.3 for the definition of a mature female leader to see what characteristics you want to adopt.

| Example of a Womanhood Rap | Write your own rap, poem, or statement below describing the way the ideal woman behaves. |
|---|---|
| To define being a woman, these steps you must follow. The truth is hard, so is the pill you must swallow. | |
| Patience is the key to big success. Having self-discipline gets rid of the stress. | |
| A grown woman accepts others and obeys the law. Respects herself and boosts healthy thoughts. | |
| She's responsible for her own actions. Earning her way gives her satisfaction. | |
| Never does she give up or promote violence. She also understands the concept of guidance. | |
| She knows the value of hugs and what drugs do to you. No, she's not self-centered nor influenced by cruel peers. She treats guys right; she's becoming a grown woman tonight. | |

One of the most important ways to be a respectable lady is to have standards, values, and ideals that place limits on what actions are acceptable and what behaviors are unsatisfactory. Different cultures have various standards for the way that mature ladies behave. The key to being an emotionally and physically healthy woman is to embrace a set of standards to uphold. Here are some examples. Which ones work best for you?

Exercise 2.2

Womanhood Development Various Codes of Conduct: DISCUSSION.
Check out these womanhood standards and see which ones work best for you.
Explain why these guidelines for being a mature woman fit your
situation.


## American Girl Scout Law

A Girl Scout is:

I will do my best to be

> honest and fair
> friendly and helpful
> considerate and caring
> courageous and strong, and
> responsible for what I say and do,
> and to
> respect myself and others
> respect authority, use resources wisely
> make the world a better place, and
> be a sister to every Girl Scout.

How well does the Girl Scout Code fit the lifestyle of young, female people today? How
would you change it to fit today's youth, or are these standards timeless? Explain why.

What are the main differences between the American Girl Scout Law and the Nguza Saba
principles?

# NGUZA SABA PRINCIPLES

## By Dr. Maulana Karenga

Unity (Umoja): To strive for and maintain unity in the family, community, nation, and race.

Self-determination (Kujichjulia): To define ourselves, name ourselves, and speak for ourselves instead of being defined and spoken for by others.

Collective work and responsibility (Ujima): To build and maintain our community together; to make our brothers' and sisters' problems our problems, and to solve these problems together.

Cooperative economics (Ujama): To build and own stores, shops and other businesses, and profit together from them.

Purpose (Nia): To make as our collective vocation the building and development of our community in order to restore people to their traditional greatness.

Creativity (Kuumba): To always do as much as we can, in the way we can, so as to leave our community more beautiful and beneficial than when we inherited it.

Faith (Imani): To believe, regardless of what others say, in our parents, our teachers, our leaders, our people, and ourselves, and the righteousness and victory of our struggle.

Exercise 2.2 Here is another code of conduct that Spelman College associates created. The code of conduct consists of the following standards:

### ♦ Civility ♦

• I contribute to a civil environment of respect and encourage inclusiveness in a manner that models free inquiry, critical thinking, and intellectual engagement.

• I am honest. I will do my own academic work. I will not lie, cheat, steal, plagiarize, forge or falsify any information.

• I am civil. I will not fight, instigate, or perpetuate discord within the community or on social networking sites.

### ♦ Commitment ♦

• I take responsibility and understand that I am accountable for my behavior, personal growth and development of character.

• I practice respect and integrity at all times as I contribute to a culture and community of excellence.

• I honor my commitments. I attend classes and activities to which I commit on time as outlined by my instructors and/or administrators, and I deliver quality outcomes in a reliable, timely, and positive manner.

• I commit to engage in respectful relationships with friends, acquaintances, roommates, classmates, faculty, administrators, staff, alumnae, guests and those outside the Spelman community on a daily basis.

• I engage in actions that affirm our sisterhood as a culture of support on a daily basis.

• I commit daily to executing my responsibilities and all that I do with an unwavering dedication to excellence.

Personal Code of Conduct of Matt Goldenberg

Matt Goldenberg is the founder of Self-Made Renegade, a career coaching firm that helps college grads and career changers get hired without the right degree, connections, or work experience.

I am the genesis of a hero, a creator, a monk, and a child. I aim to journey on, create, experience, and play with life. My core is not limited by or defined by these personality traits, rather, it limits and defines them. These traits are both prescriptive of what I can and should be at my best, and descriptive of what I cannot help but even at my worst. Life is my journey, my sanctuary, my playground, my bedroom, and above all, my creation. I am a hero. I fight for who I am and what I believe. I recognize that life is fleeting, and can end in an instant, so I consciously work to make sure I am achieving life with every breath. I know that I must work, fight, and suffer along this road; that I must do what needs to be done to learn the lessons I need, to struggle and return victorious as the hero. I seek to follow my purpose and defeat the challenges along the way. I recognize that while death is to be fought and avoided at all costs, a life without purpose is a fate worse than death.

I am a monk. I immerse myself in the experience of life in this moment. I appreciate the majesty of life as an end in itself. I hold my focus as my greatest gift, and consciously direct it to experience life. I recognize that while planning for the future and learning from the past are important, I must be willing to die at any moment, and if I die, I must die fully immersed in the present. I have an affinity with nature and with other humans, as when I am immersed in the moment, I can empathize with the rhythms of nature and the feelings of others. At all times, my deepest core is at peace, even in the presence of great outside stressors.

I am a creator. I create the world around me and within me as I see fit. I use my unlimited power and will to change the future. My will is my greatest tool with which I can create and change the world. My work ethic is unparalleled and this is what allows me to create such great works. I create things out of passion, out of joy, out of expression, things that are astounding, that express who I am, and enhance others' lives. As a creator, I know my body may die, but I will not, as I will live on in my creations, which are and always will be created in my image. I radiate a force and power tangible to all who come in contact with me. I am a woman/man who moves the world.

I am a child. I seek to immerse myself in joy and love free of self-consciousness or pretension. I play and laugh freely, drawing those around me into a state of playfulness. My imagination is endless and wonderful, my greatest tool with which to play with the world. I can direct my innocence and imagination to solve problems in a creative fashion and see simple solutions that elude others. I do not use play as a means to an end; it is an end in itself. Laughter is my greatest gift to the world and happiness is my greatest gift to myself. If I must die, I will die with laughter in my heart.

Exercise 2.2 (continued)

How do these codes of conduct compare with each other?

Which of these codes of conduct best fits the way that you are raised?

Which elements of these codes of conduct are most likely to help you become a well-rounded, sophisticated, considerate lady?

Why should every mature lady follow a code of conduct?

What do you think about the statement that every woman should follow a universal code of conduct?

How well do the following universal standards of behavior work for you?

- Treat all people with love, acceptance, and fairness.

- Treat people the way that you want to be treated.

How would your life be if everyone in the world followed this universal code of behavior?

**Exercise 2.3**
**Types of Love: SELF-ACCEPTANCE AND SELF-LOVE**
**Girlhood to Womanhood**

**Loving Yourself**

Self-love is one of the most important types of love that a person can have. This form of love is important because it is difficult, if not impossible, to care for other people passionately without loving yourself. Loving this way begins with acceptance.

One of the wisest things that you can do is to recognize that you are always going to be faced with the physical person that you are unless you get surgically altered. Therefore, you should accept the person that you are and build your womanhood on that acceptance. You must be your own best friend in order to be a leader and a fully developed woman. No circumstance, no condition, no loss in your life is worth sacrificing yours. You have an obligation as a woman and leader to become all that you can become as a person. Any self-destructive action on your part is contrary to being a mature woman and a real leader.

## Exercise 2.4
## Cultivating Sisterly Love: SKIT COMPETITION

### STEPS: What you do

- Groups of participants will create a Ujima skit on sisterly love.
- The facilitator will rate the quality of the skits.
- You will have 15 minutes to create a skit that uses the Ujima principle.
- Read the problem situation and then act out an appropriate solution to the problem.

Collective work and responsibility (Ujima) — To build and maintain our community together, to make our brothers' and sisters' problems our problems and to solve these problems together.

Ujima Problem Situation (Solving your brothers' and sisters' problems together)
You are walking home after school. You see one of your best friends in an argument with her boyfriend. At first, they are staring at each other with angry facial expressions, then they start yelling at each other. Then all of a sudden, your best friend pushes him to the ground.

In your skit, act out a peaceful way to keep this situation from getting any worse. Show how you could safely help your friend and the guy resolve this impasse and work toward a better understanding for all parties involved.

**Exercise 2.5**
**Demonstrating Concern: FOR OTHERS**

**STEPS: What you do**
1. Groups of participants will create a Umoja skit showing concern for others.
2. The facilitator will rate the quality of the skits.
3. You will have 15 minutes to create a skit that uses the Umoja principle.
4. Read the problem situation and then act out an appropriate solution to the problem.

Umoja Problem Situation (Maintain unity in family, community, nation, and race)

A teenager and her 10-year-old female neighbor are shooting hoops at the basketball court. When it's time for them to go home, the teary-eyed girl says that she doesn't want to go home because her stepfather is there. She is afraid to face her stepfather because the girl broke the stereo which she had been told not to touch.

Develop a skit that shows the conversation between the other teenager and the girl. How could you, as the teenager in this situation, show your concern in a positive manner while showing compassion and understanding for the girl and her stepfather?

**Turning Girls into Ladies**

**A Multicultural, Behavioral Approach**

**Supporting Your Peers**

**Lesson 3**

## Learning objectives

## You will learn:

- Ways to support your peers
- The meaning of the term Resiliency Networking

Exercise 3.1

## Mutual Support: FOR YOUR PEERS

### STEPS: *What you do*
*Read the passage below. Ask yourself: Do I have a responsibility to help my friends and others achieve their goals and dreams?*

## Girlhood to Womanhood

## FOUNDATION Girls and Ladies

Learning to support each other

A set of skills that a young lady can learn shows how to support and provide genuine recognition and care for other females in their age group. The teen years are a time when many youths experiment with new roles and ways of thinking. At the same time, many seek the approval and respect of others in their age group. Youth aggressively search for friendly relationships that fulfill their need for acceptance and belonging.

At the same time, once they earn membership in a circle of friends, they feel safe enough to engage in playful teasing. In some neighborhoods, the exchange can become a source of entertainment for many of the young ladies. Because of the pleasure they receive from their interaction with each other, sometimes the teasing and criticism go overboard. Part of this playfulness involves the exchange of what some would consider to be insults. At other times, the insults amount to bullying, including cyberbullying. Sometimes the insults are straightforward and designed to entertain. At other times, the insults are uncomplimentary comments that turn vicious. In all cases, a mature person who is striving to be a respectable young woman avoids mistreating others in her age group.

In the 1960s and 1970s, some young women had a similar way of exchanging insulting remarks with each other: "Joning," "Playing the Dozens," or "Scoring." Some called it "Clownin" in the Midwest and south. It was a unique and different way of forming friendships, but there are strong similarities to the verbal exchanges that sometimes occur among some girls today. This social process concentrates on being quick-witted. The more clever the young lady is at making fun of his peers, the more entertaining her comments will be to the audience of friends and peers. In this way, she gains attention, respect, and dominance over her peers.

On one level, this entertaining, but aggressive style of relating to each other, appears to be innocent in comparison to the more vicious way of talking to each other. Some young women find the experience so entertaining and appealing that they taunt and tease each other continually. They see the exchange as being harmless. On a deeper level, the young women in this situation can achieve closeness and bonding through this teasing process.

Many adolescents say there is nothing bad about participating in this lighthearted teasing. When a female becomes 25 or thirty, however, the form of building relationships can grow into a lack of respect for or distrust of other females. What was acceptable as a girl is no longer acceptable as a lady. The results can become so serious that some young ladies become isolated from each other. Others become unduly suspicious of the motives of a new female acquaintance.

This mental grooming process does not occur by itself. One argument is that the negative portrayal of some females on television, movies, and other media contributes to the lack of trust, suspicion, and separation from each other. Failure to learn to work together can place females who are affected by it at a disadvantage in their quest to become complete, mature ladies.

How can I help a friend who is in need?
Think of the following situations and fill in the spaces with positive actions you can take.

If my friend's family doesn't have enough food, I can help by:

If my classmate is sick, I can help by:

If my friend is lonely, I can help by:

If the girls in my community are skipping school, I can help by:

If my classmate is spreading gossip, I can help by:

If my classmate is starting fights, I can help by:

The real question to consider is not whether teasing and insulting your female peers, who are usually your friends, is good or bad. Instead, the real question is whether there is a better and more mature way of relating to each other. In other words, could you be wasting time and energy involved in negativity like cursing each other? Could you channel the time toward building sisterhood and encouraging other young ladies to achieve their goals and dreams together? Could you use this energy to build strong families, businesses, and communities?

The decision to promote each other's success is a learned skill, and it is one that does not necessarily come naturally. Some say that people in society often encourage negative events and negative views of events. That could include encouraging fighting and cursing at each other in movies, television, etc. as if the actions are acceptable roles to follow. Regardless of whether this is true, the situation does not have to be this way for everyone. Young ladies can reprogram themselves through self-examination and self-study. Learning effective ways to support other young ladies is a skill that every truly maturing female has a responsibility to acquire.


Exercise 3.2
The Sisterhood: SPEAKOUT GAME

STEPS: What you do

- You will break into small groups to come up with a list of 5 positive statements young girls can make about each other.

- Select a group spokesperson who will repeat your group's positive statements.

- Each group takes turns until either time or the list runs out.

| SPEAKOUT GAME STATEMENTS: |
| LIST 5 POSITIVE STATEMENTS TO DESCRIBE YOUR PEERS. |
| --- |
| 1. |
| 2. |
| 3. |
| 4. |
| 5. |

EXERCISE 3.3
RESILIENCY: The female relationship NETWORK

Steps: What you do in this exercise

Consider the following definition:

What is resiliency networking?

Working definition

    A female resiliency network involves forming positive, healthy <u>relationships</u> with girls in your age group, girls older than you, and girls younger than you. It involves reaching forward, side to side, and behind you to form a strong blanket of security, prosperity, and health. This responsibility also involves giving backing to people younger than you, helping to strengthen the community, and showing concern for the future of all people.

Exercise 3.4

**Giving back: Forming the resiliency network**

**Girlhood to Womanhood Foundation**

**Giving Back Results in Personal Satisfaction**

Learning the skill of giving back is a responsibility that girls have to themselves, one another, their community, and the institutions that serve them. Mature ladies recognize that giving back is a way to obtain personal satisfaction and a way to add a sense of meaning to their lives. Giving back is a serious responsibility that every female must assume in order to help PREVENT THE HARMFUL EFFECTS OF OTHER POSSIBLE NEGATIVE INFLUENCES LIKE HIV and hepatitis infection, and violence in society today.

WOMANHOOD REQUIREMENT

GIVE BACK TO TWO YOUNG PEOPLE AND REQUIRE THEM TO DO THE SAME WITH TWO YOUNGER THAN THEM. IN THIS WAY, TWO WOMANHOOD TRAINEES BECOME FOUR, FOUR BECOME EIGHT, EIGHT BECOME 16.... THE NUMBER INCREASES IN THIS WAY TO BUILD THOUSANDS AND PERHAPS MILLIONS OF POSITIVE AND HEALTHY RELATIONSHIPS.

## 3.5
**Building a Resiliency Network**

**STEPS: What you do**
**Study the following definition:**

INTEGRITY: The demonstration of trustworthiness, uprightness, and dedication to doing what is right regardless of pressures to do otherwise.

CHARACTER: The display of high regard for standards of behavior without the need for monitoring from others; moral self-control and discipline; the ability to keep a good reputation by following social rules, laws, and guidelines for the benefit of all people.

DECENCY: The expression of high morals and principles for living your life; exhibiting proper actions toward others according to a standard of courtesy for living with respect for other people.

Exercise 3.6
Complaining About Others VERSUS TAKING CHARGE

Girlhood to Womanhood FOUNDATION PASSAGE

Choose a Clear Vision

Setting Goals, Goal Getting

Too many young females may want to place responsibility for their achievement on someone else. It is a sign of immaturity. The full and final responsibility for your success lies with you. Every person on this planet has a burden of some kind to bear. Older people must overcome barriers as they age. Overweight people face the challenge of dealing with issues of health and others who mock or mistreat them because of their size. Some people who have a particular religious belief have to cope with discrimination and prejudice simply because of their faith.

A young lady has two ways that she can respond to unfavorable conditions. She can choose to complain and become a victim of a situation, or she can choose to use the situation to motivate herself to overcome obstacles. Blaming people, foreigners, women, or others for her present condition is counterproductive.

**Exercise 3.7**

# WOMANHOOD SUCCESS PLAN

**Name:** _____

Complete YOUR plan for success in life by following the examples below. Least each item in detail.

| SITUATIONS FOR GOAL SETTING | PROPOSED ACTION | MEASURABLE SUCCESS MARKER | DEADLINE |
|---|---|---|---|
| Example 1. In my school, | I will completely fill out | two applications for computer training program on building construction | by June 1, of a selected year (such as, 2050) |
| 1. In my personal life, | I will | | by (date). |
| 2. In my personal life, | I will | | by (date). |
| 3. In my family, | I will | | by (date). |
| 4. In school, | I will | | by (date). |
| 5. With my friends, | I will | | by (date). |
| 6. In my community, | I will | | by (date). |

Blaming others does not serve any reasonable purpose because it wastes energy that could be used to become successful. Recognize that any negative influence from other people is temporary. A determined young lady has the power she needs to overcome negative people and events in her life. All she has to do is choose to use this power to her advantage. Let people who create obstacles for her serve as a motivating influence.

Exercise 3.7

A young woman's energy is a precious commodity. The energy she puts into complaining and blaming others is the energy that she could use to move forward as a leader in life. The greatest challenge that she has is getting a clear vision of the successful female leader that she wants to become.

The next step is to establish important goals with specific dates for accomplishing them. For example, a young lady might want to own a home building business with a goal of building 100 homes per year, beginning 10 years from today. (Remember to write into the goals the exact month, day, and year for accomplishing these goals.)

She decides what it will take for her to achieve the goal. She monitors her progress toward the attainment of skills or resources to achieve each goal. She does not wait for anyone else to check her success as she works toward her goals. She checks herself at least weekly and writes down how far she has progressed toward her targets.

> **THIS IS AN IMPORTANT PART OF BEING A WOMAN WHO IS SERIOUS ABOUT BECOMING SUCCESSFUL.**

> **USE RESILIENCY NETWORKING TO WEAVE TOGETHER A HEALTHIER PLACE TO LIVE FOR EVERYONE. THIS IS AN IMPORTANT PART OF BEING AN AUTHENTIC WOMAN WHO IS A GENUINE LEADER.**

# Turning Girls into Ladies
## A Multicultural, Behavioral Approach

## Health and Fitness

## Lesson 4

## Lesson 4

**Learning objectives**

You will learn about:
- Healthy eating patterns.
- Ways in which exercise helps to maintain optimum health.
- Ways in which healthy eating and exercise work hand-in-hand to promote healthy living.
- Stress reduction

**Exercise 4.1**
## CONDITIONING FOR OPTIMAL HEALTH

## GIRLHOOD TO WOMANHOOD

**Your Health is Your Wealth**
**Eat to live, don't just live to eat.**

## BOYHOOD TO MANHOOD

## FOUNDATION

Have you ever thought about how important it is to take care of your body? Does eating a balanced meal, maintaining a weight that is age, body type, and height appropriate mean anything to you? Young females must address these questions head-on without taking it too far. A healthy individual is one who works to improve all aspects of herself. One area of a person's life must not be neglected for the other. Understanding the best ways to become mature inside and outside, from top to bottom, all parts of who she is must move toward top condition to maintain ideal health and the best possible level of success in life. The goal for maturing females is to begin to understand better the importance of taking care of your entire self. Young people sometimes experience diseases and health conditions just as older people, but they can stop many health problems in their tracks by taking excellent care of themselves. This is a core part of being a responsible, mature lady.

According to the U.S. Centers for Disease Control and Prevention (CDC), as much as 33% of young people are overweight (obese). How can you keep this from becoming a problem for you? Good nutrition is necessary in order to provide fuel for the body and nutrients for proper body functioning.

Guidelines for healthy eating continue to change as we learn more about good eating practices. The CDC continually updates its recommendations about good eating habits based on scientific findings. Some recent recommendations are listed in a brochure called "Choose Your Plate." Here are some of their recommendations:

**Centers for Disease Control & Prevention — Nutritional Recommendations**

- Make half your plate fruits and vegetables.
- Eat red, orange, and dark-green vegetables, such as tomatoes, sweet potatoes, and broccoli, in main and side dishes.
- Eat fruit, vegetables, or unsalted nuts as snacks - they are nature's original fast foods. Switch to skim or 1% milk. (They have the same amount of calcium and other essential nutrients as whole milk, but less fat and calories.)
- Try calcium-fortified soy products as an alternative to dairy foods.
- Make at least half your grains whole.
- Choose 100% wholegrain cereals, breads, crackers, rice, and pasta.
- Check the ingredients list on food packages to find whole-grain foods. Vary your protein food choices.
- Twice a week, make seafood the protein on your plate.
- Eat beans, which are a natural source of fiber and protein.
- Keep meat and poultry portions small and lean. Keep your food safe to eat.

Learn more at www.FoodSafety.gov.

A well-rounded young person has the responsibility of keeping up with these changing recommendations as she grows into ladyhood and beyond this transition. Young females need to take in only the number of calories that experts say is healthy. Overeating is unhealthy like under-eating. Record how much food you eat daily and stay within that amount. Scientific studies support the fact that eating the right amount of food may help you to live longer. Young ladies have to be careful in this way to live a long, high-quality life.

**Food for Thought**

1. How well do these guidelines fit with the way that you lead your life?
2. What would you need to do to change the way that you live in order to comply with these guidelines?
3. How willing are you to eat like this?
4. What does good nutrition and exercise have to do with being a well-rounded lady?

**Exercise 4.2**
**STRESS MANAGEMENT AND ITS EFFECT ON LADYHOOD**

**What do you think about ways to handle stress in your life?**

Often we think of health in terms of our physical wellbeing, but mental health is just as important. One area of mental health with which young ladies should be concerned is stress. Stress plagues many people. How do we effectively deal with the discomfort of the pressures of life? How do we cope with this uneasiness that is often associated with stress? How do healthy young people deal with societal stressors that affect people, especially male youth?

It is important to identify the source of discomfort. This usually happens through a problem-solving process or a process of elimination of less desirable life choices. Although it is not always possible to determine why a young lady feels the way he does, one effective way to handle stress is through exercise.

Exercise helps to relieve tension and promote relaxation after a hard workout. It is important to maintain a bodyweight that is appropriate for your physical size, height, and bone structure. It is easier to burn calories and reduce stress when you are fit. You can move a trim and lean body more smoothly.

A life with less stress can help keep your blood pressure lower, and you are likely to eat less food unnecessarily. This helps you to be less prone to heart attacks and strokes ("brain attacks") as you get older. Sometimes a young lady who deviates from a healthy nutrition plan uses food as a comforter. Talking to a counselor, parents, or a responsible and trustworthy confidant can be an effective way to keep stress at a level that is low enough so that eating to offset stress is far less necessary.

Young people are often vulnerable to unintended injuries. Therefore, it makes sense to be prepared if an unexpected injury occurs. Remember that being in peak mental and physical condition can help you recover from unintentional injuries like car accidents, sports injuries, falls, or other unhealthy events.

**Discussion Questions**

1. What is a "brain attack" or stroke?
2. How is a "brain attack" like a heart attack?
3. How well-equipped do you think you are to handle stress in your life?
4. What measures do you think you will need to take to respond to stress in life as you get older?
5. What are the most important sources of stress in your life?

6. How can you prevent the most important stressors in your life from interfering with the way that you live?

7. What does managing stress have to do with becoming a mature, well-rounded lady?

**Exercise 4.3**

**The Body, Food, and Fuel: Comparison to a Luxury Car**

Think about a car as a model for ways that your body uses food or fuel. Understanding how to consume and burn the right food in your body is as important as maintaining the right gas and oil in a car. The car has a metal frame that houses all of its parts and so does our body have a physical frame. It is important that all the parts of your body work well together just as the parts of the car do when they are well maintained. The car requires a tune-up, oil change, air filter, gas filter, and air in the tires periodically.

Likewise, your body needs food, water, rest, vitamins, and exercise to run smoothly. The body functions better when the heart can pump blood throughout the body with ease. Just as the car's fuel pump sends a flow of gasoline to the engine to burn in order to make it run, the heart must pump fuel easily. The car stores fuel in the gas tank while humans store our energy source in our digestive system initially.

When additional energy is needed, the car pulls from its gasoline reserves to keep it moving. The body draws its energy from the food taken in daily. When the energy level falls short, the fuel reserve which the fat cells store is used to keep the body going. The engine is the heart of the car, and it has to run smoothly or the rest of the car will not function properly. The same applies to the heart. It cannot beat and pump blood effectively if it is clogged with cholesterol and plaque deposits.

The tires on the car represent the arms and legs of the human in this example. The tires are needed for movement. The legs and arms are used for the movement of our bodies. The tires must remain inflated properly, and the muscles must be toned and in good working order for a young lady like you to walk, grasp objects, and carry items efficiently.

The body is perfectly made and requires that a young leader gives it the best attention she can to be healthy in all areas. Mental health requires a healthy body to function the way it is intended. We do not think very well if we have had too little sleep, for example. Loving ourselves enough to take care of our mental health is a very important step for a person to take to lead friends, family, and the community in a positive direction.

Discussion Questions

1. Which parts of this comparison of a car to the way your body works makes the most sense to you? Explain why.
2. What is your responsibility as a woman for seeing to it that all aspects of elements that affect your health fit well together?
3. How can you work with your family and friends to keep you in line with these recommendations for nutrition, exercise, and stress management?
4. What are some ways that you can use computer applications and devices to keep a record of your health habits?
5. How can you use this information to reach health goals?

## Exercise 4.4

**This form is an example of a food intake recording tool. Read it carefully. Consider using electronic methods to save this information.**

| Table 1.<br>The Healthy Lady<br>A Day's Food Intake Record |
| --- |
| Write down what you ate and how much.<br>Breakfast<br>I ate the following foods:<br>1. _____ 2. _____ 3. _____ 4. _____ 5. |
| Write down what you ate and how much.<br>Breakfast<br>I ate the following foods:<br>1. _____ 2. _____ 3. _____ 4. _____ 5. |
| Write down what you ate and how much.<br>Snack<br>I ate the following foods:<br>1. _____ 2. _____ 3. _____ 4. _____ 5. |
| Write down what you ate and how much.<br>Lunch<br>I ate the following foods:<br>1. _____ 2. _____ 3. _____ 4. _____ 5. |

Write down what you ate and how much.
Snack
I ate the following foods:
1. _____ 2. _____ 3. _____ 4. _____ 5.
_____

Write down what you ate and how much.
Dinner
I ate the following foods:
1. _____ 2. _____ 3. _____ 4. _____ 5.
_____

Write down what you ate and how much.
Snack before bedtime
I ate the following foods:
1. _____ 2. _____ 3. _____ 4. _____ 5.
_____

### Exercise 4.4

**Your Body: HOW FIT ARE YOU?**

**STEPS:** *What you do*
*The group leader will give you directions for the following class activities.*

**Mini-fitness Course**
(Make sure that your doctor says that it is fine for you to perform this exercise before doing it.) Set up an exercise space in a room. Do exercises like basic muscle toning, aerobics, and flexibility. Describe what body responses would tell you that you are in shape or out of shape. What do you think you should do about what you learn from this process?

**Healthy Taste Testing Party**
Have a taste testing party. Consider making healthy smoothies. (Make sure that no one has any food allergies or conditions that would prevent them from eating specific foods like nuts, vegetables, etc.) Consider making smoothies with fruits and vegetables. Bring in fruits, vegetables, nuts, and other healthy foods for participants to sample. Gather health foods to sample during the party. Take a vote among the group participants to see which health foods and recipes are the most popular winners among the samples for the day.

**Stress Reducer**

Learn alternatives for reducing stress through problem-solving.

**Problem-Solving Steps**

1.  Define what the problem is.
2.  List possible solutions to the problem.
3.  Consider the costs and benefits associated with each solution.
4.  Select a solution.
5.  Put the solution into action
6.  Check to see if the solution really solved the problem.
7.  Start over again if necessary.

Note, however, that the best approach is to prevent life problems from taking place BEFORE they happen. Many of life's problems have preventive solutions if you find out what the solutions are and use them well.

### Role Play

### Two Friends' Stress indicators

Role-play the following scenario and discuss various problem-solving steps.

*Michelle and Janet have been friends since kindergarten. Lately, it seems Janet has been unusually quiet and eats all the time. She is obviously gaining weight in her stomach and other parts of her body. Michelle is worried because she has never seen her friend act like this before. Michelle decides to ask Janet if there is a problem, but Janet acts as if she is offended when confronted. How can Michelle help Janet resolve her eating problem without making Janet feel bad?*

### Exercise 4.5

### Food Consumption: WHAT AM I EATING?

**What you do in this exercise**

1.  Create a food diary by filling in the blanks in Table 1 with the food items that you ate yesterday.

2.  How difficult is it to remember this information?

3.  How else can you keep an accurate record with your computer, cell phone, or other handheld devices?

4.  What computer programs or "apps" can you use for this purpose?

5.  How would you use these computer-based solutions for monitoring your health habits?

# Turning Girls into Ladies
## A Multicultural, Behavioral Approach

## Male-Female Relationships

## Lesson 5

**Turning Girls into Ladies**

**A Multicultural, Behavioral Approach**

**Male-Female Relationships**

**Lesson 5**

### Learning Objectives

You should learn about the qualities of:

- A perfect lady?
- The type of man that ladies want?
- An ideal relationship.

### Exercise 5.1
**Identifying the Ideal and LESS THAN IDEAL MATE**
(Provide a 2-3 sentence description.)

_____

_____

_____

_____

### Exercise 5.2
**Let's talk about MALE-FEMALE RELATIONSHIPS**

MY MALE-FEMALE RELATIONSHIP STRENGTHS
LIST 3 GOOD PERSONALITY QUALITIES THAT YOU POSSESS:

1.

2.

3.

MY MALE-FEMALE RELATIONSHIP GROWTH AREAS:

_____

_____

_____

_____

LIST 3 LESS PREFERRED WAYS OF ACTING THAT YOU USE FOR GETTING ALONG WITH MALES:

1.

2.

3.

**Exercise 5.3**
**Healthy and Unhealthy INTIMATE (GIRLFRIEND-BOYFRIEND) RELATIONSHIPS**

WHAT THINGS ABOUT YOUR BEHAVIOR WOULD A MALE FIND HEALTHY IN A RELATIONSHIP?

CONSIDER YOUR PAST CONDUCT IN SOME OF YOUR RELATIONSHIPS AND LIST THREE GOOD BEHAVIORS. (USE OTHER PEOPLE'S RELATIONSHIPS AS EXAMPLES IF NECESSARY.)

1.

2.

3.

WHAT THINGS ABOUT YOU WOULD A MALE FIND UNHEALTHY IN A RELATIONSHIP?

CONSIDER YOUR PAST CONDUCT IN SOME OF YOUR RELATIONSHIPS AND LIST THREE CHALLENGING BEHAVIORS THAT CAUSED PROBLEMS IN YOUR GETTING ALONG WITH EACH OTHER:

1.

2.

3.

**Exercise 5.4**
**Components of INTIMATE RELATIONSHIPS**

**Girlhood to Womanhood**

Healthy Relationships
One + One

- In healthy relationships, each person is satisfied enough with herself to be comfortable without the company of another person. (Each person enjoys time alone occasionally for some couples.)
- Both parties complement the other or make the other person stronger as an individual.
- They strengthen the accomplishments of each other and help the other mate to perform better.
- They anticipate the needs of the other person and gladly respond to the other person's needs without showing a negative attitude or resentment.
- They resist the desire to hold onto old conflicts, arguments, and sensitive points.
- Both partners let go of hard feelings that always spring up in any relationship between two people.
- They are willing to forgive the other person for making mistakes.
- Each partner has one mate and remains committed to maintaining a relationship with one person at a time. This means that a mature female (or male) who wants to exercise leadership in building her intimate relationship resists the temptation to pursue other individuals who are outside of a loving relationship.
- Recognize that marriage and children may not be for everyone because of the great deal of commitment and sacrifice that is required to maintain healthy relationships and to care for children. This is an individual commitment aimed at protecting each person in the marriage and each child resulting from the marriage.
- Understand that no partner is going to be perfect. Each mate, therefore, has to be willing to overlook the imperfections of the other person or be willing to resolve impasses.
- Each person must be willing to talk through misunderstandings and to reach agreeable solutions for both partners.

How do you measure up on these items that are designed to promote healthy relationships?

_____

_____

_____

_____

_____

- Neither person in a relationship can control the other person's life. One partner must be willing to let the other person grow and develop to the fullest degree possible.
- Trust in the relationship is essential. Each partner must be trustworthy and trusting. Consequently, a healthy relationship is one where either person can spend time with male or female friends without their partner worrying about threats to the intimacy of the relationship.
- Both partners have to be comfortable with the fact that their partner's relationship with friends and family is an acceptable, if not a necessary way for a partner to be a whole person. Whenever one partner wants to cut the other partner off completely from friends and family, this is a sign that the relationship is not healthy. Maintaining an unhealthy relationship may not be worth the effort of either person.
- Physical conflict (e.g., hitting) and mental abuse (e.g., being exceptionally critical and insulting) is a sign that the relationship is in trouble. Partners who engage in either behavior may actually be little girls, or little boys for that matter, who are trapped in a grown woman's or man's body. They can be 30, 40, 50, or 60 years old and still be teenagers as far as their leadership and emotional maturity level is concerned in their relationships.
- Always be willing to seek professional help to promote a healthy relationship. This kind of support may occur as the relationship changes over the years. Partners need to stay flexible enough to view the process of seeking relationship counseling as a strength. Multiple Simultaneous Relationships Pose Great Emotional and Health Risks
- The gold standard for female-male relationships may be staying with one mate at a time. Dating other men while you are in a relationship with one person is often not a good option. There is nothing cool or lady-like about running from one man to the next. Today, having multiple relationships at the same time can pose a great health risk, or possibly become a handicapping condition or a death sentence because of diseases like HIV/AIDS. Using a condom is safer than unprotected sex. Abstinence, or not having sex at all, is the

safest way to protect yourself. Always protect yourself and others from sexual diseases. Untreated, these diseases can kill. The more sexual partners you have, the more likely it is that you can acquire a disease. Real women are often strong and wise enough to remain faithful to one person.

**Make a list that tells which of the items just described fits with your lifestyle. Explain how you can fulfill the expectations described in this passage. What challenges do you see with becoming a woman who meets these expectations?**

_____

_____

_____

## Exercise 5.5
## Healthy Relationships Help People Grow

Bragging about the number of males with whom you have had sex is a sign of immaturity. Sexual intercourse should be a private experience between two people. It should not be shared with best friends or acquaintances. Both parties can grow and become better people when one person helps the other person to deal with life's problems. Remember, you may be placing yourself at risk of being handicapped or dying by having close relationships and exchanging body fluids with several males at a time. Aside from the health risks of dating multiple partners at the same time, it can lead to other social conflicts, including physical violence because of jealousy. Learning to be a strong and wise woman helps to improve your relationship with your mate.

**What would you say to other males to teach them about these points? What are the most important items presented in this passage above?**

**What are the safest relationships: Having no sex?**

Besides contracting HIV, other health dangers include hepatitis (liver disease) and causing pregnancy through unprotected sex. Unprotected sex can cause death in today's society. The safest sexual behavior is no sex at all that could result in an exchange of body fluids. As a leader, you need to learn how to communicate with your mate. You can make it your business to communicate about issues like abstinence (not having sex) and using condoms to prevent the transmission of body fluids that carry the viruses. Be familiar with the behaviors that can make it more likely for you to catch viruses. Examples include having multiple sex partners and exchanging body fluids by any means during any sex act.

Any time you risk getting someone pregnant, you place your life at risk for dying early of HIV/AIDS and other serious diseases when untreated. The most serious problem that females with multiple sex partners face is the fact that they are frequently at greater risk for catching HIV or sexually transmitted infections (STIs) during unprotected sex compared to many other people who protect themselves. Examples of protecting yourself include being abstinent (no intimate sexual behavior) and using condoms correctly. (Condoms can fail, however, but many experts believe that they are better than using no protection.) You can avoid being the victim of the deadly HIV virus or other STIs by being the smart one in the situation. Remember anyone, a friend, mate or otherwise, who would expose you to catching the virus is not really your friend. A real friend will never expose you to HIV, STIs, or interfere with your success. Know your friends. A mature lady avoids dangerous people and hazardous situations.

**Write down what you would tell your friends to get them to understand how serious these issues are? How would you get them to protect themselves from these problems?**

_____

_____

_____

_____

_____

_____

# Turning Girls into Ladies
## A Multicultural, Behavioral Approach

## Respect for Men (Part 1)

## Lesson 6

**Turning Girls into Ladies**

**A Multicultural, Behavioral Approach**

**Respect for Men (Part 1)**

**Lesson 6**

## WORDS CAN SHOW RESPECT
## WHAT HARM ARE YOU CAUSING WITH YOUR WORDS?

**Female-Roles**

**Learning Objectives**

You should learn:

• How to acknowledge guys by using positive, respectful, and complimentary statements toward them.

• Mutual support between ladies and men in various relationships: sibling, friendship, coworker, and dating.

**Exercise 6.1**
**Using Words that show guys reasonable respect**

STEPS: What you do:

Use Table 6.1 on the next page to identify words that could be considered respectful or disrespectful to males.

*Just as guys need to show respect for girls, girls need to respect guys as well as equals.*

**Exercise 6.2**
**Gauging Reactions from the opposite sex**

STEPS: What you do:

Think about the following questions and be prepared to discuss them with the group.

1. How do guys usually respond when you use words from list A toward them?
2. How do boys respond when you use words from list B toward them?
3. Do the participants who use words from list B toward their mothers also use words from this list toward their boyfriends and other male friends?
   (A girl who disrespects her parents may also disrespect her mate, lover, boyfriend, etc.)
4. Do you feel good when you have used words from list B toward some young man in your life?
5. Does it make you feel more like a lady to use these words? Why or why not?
6. Is it important for you to feel in total control of young men? Why?

49

Table 6.1

| Positive Verbal Comments toward Guys | | Negative Verbal Comments toward Guys | |
|---|---|---|---|
| List A List 6 words that you can say to show respect in each space below. | | List B List 6 words that you can say to show disrespect in each space below. | |
| 1. | 2. | 1. | 2. |
| 3. | 4. | 3. | 4. |
| 5. | 6. | 5. | 6. |

## Exercise 6.3
## Portrayal of FEMALES ON T.V., IN MUSIC, AND ON THE RADIO

Women in the Media
Consider ways that the mass media—movies, T.V., magazines, music videos, songs—present images of women. Write a brief comment about your beliefs for each statement.

How are women usually portrayed respectfully in the media listed above?

What television shows, movies, or music that you listen to present women in a positive light?

What television shows, movies, or music that you listen to show women in a negative way?

In what way does it affect the way you feel to see women portrayed negatively or disrespectfully? Explain what you mean by your answer.

To what degree do you consider it to be funny in situations where women are presented in a demeaning or disrespectful way?

Write down the title of a song that uses words that are disrespectful toward women.

Think of a major role for a female in a movie with a female as a principal character. Describe the ways in which the moviemaker presented the female character positively or favorably.

What was it about the presentation of any of the females in that movie or others that you know that you considered being a negative or disrespectful representation of women? Please explain the reason for your answer in detail.

**Exercise 6.4**

## SHOWING RESPECT FOR PEOPLE OF THE OPPOSITE GENDER

Write a short description of a role in a movie that your favorite female actress could play which highlights her personal strengths and positive points. First, list at least three of her personal qualities. (Examples: brave, fearless, and considerate.) Write 2-3 paragraphs that show the actions that she takes which would cause the audience to view her as a positive character in the movie.

How does the character that you just described compare with other females in your life? What responsibility do females have to make sure that guys treat them with respect?

What can you do to help females you care about to become more like the positive character that you just described?

## Exercise 6.5
### How do You Treat BOYS?

### Girlhood to Womanhood

### Connecting the Right Way with Guys Instead of Being Abusive

One of the most important duties that a girl can fulfill is to lead other girls in connecting with guys in a way that helps both young men and women to become better people. No matter what age or behavior, one of the female leader's roles is to promote the successful and healthy lifestyle of all young people, guys, and girls. Females are not lesser individuals in any way and deserve equal treatment as partners in life. Yet one of the continuing problems that many girls and women sometimes face is mistreatment from males. Any mistreatment of women, regardless of whether it is just one time, is one time too often. Some guys think it makes them more of a man and better respected if they try to dominate or mistreat women. In reality, the reverse is true. Strong men see strong women as a complement to helping both people become better people and more successful. They are, therefore, not threatened if the female makes more money or does work that men often do. Females can play a key role in connecting with guys and showing young men how to respect girls while becoming better young men. Girls have a right to stand up for themselves in a relationship or friendship with males. The best approach is to be assertive without being abusive in standing up for yourself. That means being serious and strong in communicating your concerns without being mean or insulting. Feel free to stand up for yourself in the right way as a lady!

### How can you persuade other females and males to adopt this way of thinking?

Part of showing respect for males and protecting them is stopping the mistreatment that they are likely to experience in some situations. Yes, males can also be sexual abuse survivors in some relationships. This mistreatment includes treating males as if their only purpose in life is to satisfy females' sexual desires. It may be acceptable to admire a guy's physical attractiveness or the way that he dresses. Treating guys as sex objects to be taken advantage of is not acceptable. Females have a right to stand up for themselves and show young men how to treat them properly.

**What can you do as a female to help stop other girls from being sexually assaulted without getting hurt yourself?**

_____

_____

Examples of Solutions:

- Educate female friends about their role in treating guys appropriately.
- Talk to other girls about what treatment to accept from boyfriends or other males. (No female deserves mistreatment like being made fun of, hit, or called names.)
- Stand by female friends when they need it.
- Seek out wise counsel like a caring adult to help address the problem.

It is simply wrong for females (or guys) to yell out at the other gender with sexual overtones when this person is just walking down the street, minding his or her own business. It is inappropriate to yell at the person disrespectfully as if the person is not a person worthy of courteous treatment. Why? It is not right because too often the girls, or women, do not like it. It can make them feel very uncomfortable. People are not sex objects, and treating them courteously is essential.

Just because a female walking down the street is attractive does not give young men the right to treat them like a target of unwelcome sexual advances. Many young people who respect themselves do not feel comfortable when other people treat them like sexual "things." Young ladies and men instead deserve to be regarded as the valuable people who they are. They just happen to be there walking down the street. Regardless of whether you are 12, 21, or 70-years-old, only people who have a grade-school way of thinking and have a little girl or boy mentality disrespect others by yelling at them on the street. YOU DO NOT HAVE TO TOLERATE "CAT CALLS!" You owe it to yourself to let immature people know that you do not appreciate "cat calls," like "Hey baby! or What's up sugar?" if rude, uninvited public commentary is embarrassing or unpleasant. You can ignore them, and when the right time comes, let them know in a thoughtful and civil way that they have crossed a line of respect. Make sure that you ALWAYS exercise caution by avoiding interaction with unreasonable people by contacting the appropriate authorities if necessary. Engaging in conflict with unreasonable people is not worth it.

Yet, girls and guys have a right to show young men how important it is for young ladies to be able to get around the community without harassment from shamelessly immature people. A woman or man with self-respect does not want to be associated with a person who harasses others. BE CAREFUL WHO YOU ALLOW IN YOUR LIFE! Young ladies can inform other young ladies and men that no decent female is likely to be attracted to an immature person who insults females with "cat calls" or by any other immature and unhealthy form of mistreatment.

Ideally, this kind of treatment is not something that your close male acquaintances should ever exhibit. Think about ways to educate your male associates so that they understand their responsibility as young men to treat all females with kindness and consideration. Girls likewise have the same responsibility to treat guys in a civil manner. Shouting at each other with profanity and disrespect is never acceptable behavior for girls or guys when they hang out with or encounter each other. When females refer to other young women with profanity, like the B----. word, this is just as bad.

What would you do to convince your friends to leave alone a person who is minding her or his own business walking down the street alone when the person passes a group of "cat callers?"

_____

_____

_____

**From Girlhood to Becoming a Dignified Lady**
**Standing Up for Other Females against Sexual Assault**
**Unacceptable Advances**

Consider joining with guys who understand and embrace their responsibility to treat young women with the utmost respect, not as sex objects. A vitally important responsibility that a real lady shows is leadership in self-control and standing up for females when other males try to pressure females into having sex. Trying to force people to have sex against their will is coercion and totally unacceptable arm twisting.

Girls can educate males about the need for males to protect and stand up for girls and remember that most of the sexual mistreatment of young ladies comes from other young men. Nine and one-half times out of 10 that a female reports sexual mistreatment, a male was the person at fault. As many as one in three females have been sexually assaulted or molested in their lifetimes. One in five guys experiences sexual assault. It is criminal behavior to take advantage of people sexually when they do not want sexual advances.

**What additional supportive statements can you share with your mate and your friends who tell you that when an associate says "no" to sex, the person really means "yes?" How can you convince them that saying "no" really means "yes" is a <u>totally</u> false conclusion?**

_____

_____

Forced sex is completely unacceptable as a means for young people to grow into adulthood because that is _not_ really growing. Instead, it is just another way to remain stuck in adolescence. Girls simply _do not_ have to accept this mistreatment, and they have a responsibility to themselves to stand up for themselves against sexual assault. All people, male or female, must feel safe and free from being a sexual victim in order for them to reach their full potential as adults.

Most importantly, a female should not be forced into having sex when she does not want it. Remember that "No" means "No," regardless of when a female or male says it. Being sexually overbearing against a girl's or boy's will is totally unacceptable. This is regardless of whether the person waits one-half second before trying to get the person to change her or his mind and goes ahead and attempts or completes the sex act anyway.

**Why do many guys and girls think that it's acceptable to do the following?**

- **Force females and males to have sex**

  _____

- **Have sex with a female or male who has mental problems**

  _____

- **Try to have sex with a female or male who is passed out drunk**

  _____

**Exercise 6.6**
**Sexual Treatment and Legal Protection of Women**

**ACCEPTABLE LEGAL TREATMENT OF WOMEN**
READ THE STATEMENT AND DETERMINE IF IT IS LEGAL OR ILLEGAL.
PLACE A CHECKMARK TO THE RIGHT.

**Explain why a young person could face criminal charges if the young aggressor made the improper choice in each of the following situations.**

**Illegal**

1. It is OK to have sex with a female who has passed out in your bed. (What is wrong with this situation? Write your answer below.)

   _____

2. The person says, "I'm not that kind of girl (or guy). Leave me alone!" The sexual bully insists on taking her or his clothes off when the victim is constantly telling the bully to stop. (What is wrong with this situation?)

   _____

3. A young woman's friends tell a young lady that a guy told them he wanted to have sex with her. A few minutes later, she is alone with him, he starts unbuttoning his shirt, and she tries to run out of the room. (What is wrong with this situation?)

   _____

4. The girl is 18 and the young man is 15. She comes right out and says that she definitely wants to have sex with him. (What is wrong with this situation?)

   _____

5. The girl is 25 years old making sexual advances with a mentally challenged male student. (What is wrong with this situation?)

---

**Exercise 6.7**
**Forcible RAPE**

**WHAT IS A LEGAL DEFINITION OF RAPE?**

In the space below, write what you believe is the legal definition of rape.

How does the following definition compare with the definition that you wrote? Explain why you wrote your answer.

"Penetration, no matter how slight, of the vagina or anus with any body part or object, or oral penetration by a sex organ of another person, without the consent of the victim."

Source: Federal Bureau of Investigation (FBI), Uniform Crime Reports

**Exercise 6.8**
**Prevention of SEXUAL ASSAULT STEPS: What you do.**

It is always important to think about ways to avoid moral and legal trouble involving innocent young ladies or young men because of unwise sexual choices from sexual bullies. There is no reason to blame yourself for becoming a survivor of this sexual assault. Getting in trouble for sexual wrongdoing as a sexual bully is avoidable by thinking before the fact and doing the right thing in a circumstance like this. LEARN TO BE THE SMART ONE IN SITUATIONS LIKE THIS.

In the space following the description, write how you would handle these situations so that you can keep people from accusing you of sexual wrongdoing with a young person.

**Turning Girls into Ladies**

**A Multicultural, Behavioral Approach**

**Respect for Men (PART 2)**

**Lesson 7**

**Turning Girls into Ladies**

**A Multicultural, Behavioral Approach**

**Respect for women (PART 2)**

**Lesson 7**

## LEARNING OBJECTIVE
**You should learn:**

- Four ways to express a greater understanding of how to treat young men or let them treat you.
- One way to show how young men have a responsibility to show appreciation for females.
- Three ways to support females.
- Two ways to promote a peaceful relationship.

## Exercise 7.1
## Dealing with Friends Who MISTREAT MALE FRIENDS SEXUALLY

**STEPS: What you do**

Read the situation and answer the following question.

Imagine that you are a young lady on a camping trip with her friends. A couple of them decide to raid one of the tents on the other side of the campground. Two boys are in the tent. The young ladies' friends decide that they are going to hold the girls captive in the tent until they perform a sex act.

**Girlhood to Ladyhood**
**Property: Inappropriate Treatment of Males**

It is a female leader's responsibility to insure that guys are treated with dignity and respect, and all young ladies have a responsibility to be leaders in this way. Treating males like objects or sex toys can make it more likely that males, in turn, will victimize females. Treating males like property can lead some males to physically and sometimes mentally injure females. When you treat a person like you own them, you are more likely to act as if the person has no rights or feelings. Girls likewise have the same responsibility always to treat males with kindness and consideration.

**What Right Do Young Ladies Have to Treat Males Like Sex Objects?**

Young ladies who want to be leaders or role models will not treat guys like second class citizens either. Instead, the female leader has two roles to play. One role is as a supporter of a young man with whom she is in a family relationship - marriage, brother-sister, or father-daughter. The other role is as an opponent of injustice toward young men. Yes, young men can be survivors of sexual and other forms of abuse. The young lady in this role is willing to stand beside a young man in his defense, especially when she is with her peers. She speaks out against verbal, physical, sexual or other types of abuse of males when called for.

The female leader views males as equal partners with valuable opinions, thoughts, and points of view. Equally important, the female leader encourages equality and avoids treating males like greater or lesser human beings. She recognizes that attempting to be fair and even-handed in her treatment of male and female peers actually enriches her own standing as a human being. She is not threatened by strong males or females but rather welcomes their strength as a complement to her personal qualities. She is willing to stand up for a female's position when she is right and challenges other females in a tactful way when they make insulting remarks about males.

A healthy relationship between a male and a female is usually going to have high and low points. Miscommunications between young men and ladies are inevitable from time to time. Neither person in the relationship is always correct. Most importantly, however, each partner is willing to forgive and tries to see the other person's point of view. Neither person holds on to negative memories about the other person's mistakes or shortcomings. A strong female leader is willing to own her mistakes in a relationship.

The strong female does not tolerate being insulted, mistreated, or talked down to by young men. At the same time, she is not overly sensitive to worthwhile feedback from males. She is honest with herself about feedback from males and makes healthy adjustments in her behavior when necessary. She requires her male associates to be equally honest with themselves and make changes in their actions when necessary.

**NOTES**

_____

_____

_____

_____

_____

## Exercise 7.2
## Showing Respect to Mothers

STEPS: What you do
The facilitator will select participants to role-play the following scenario.

You have just walked into the house after being out with your friends. Your mother asks you if you saw the $10 bill that she had left on top of her bedroom dresser. (One participant will act as mother and another as you, her daughter). Show a role play where the daughter is respectful in the way she answers her mother even though she feels wrongly accused without becoming aggressive.

## <u>Exercise 7.3</u>
## Letter of Appreciation

Write an appreciation letter here addressed to the young men that you care about in your life. Explain why you regard them highly. List the positive actions that they have taken on your behalf, and find a creative way to say thank you to them in your letter. (Use a separate sheet of paper if necessary.)

Dear [Name of a great male in your life]

_____

_____

_____

_____

_____

_____

_____

Your signature here: _____

### Exercise 7.4
**Choosing How to Treat Females**

**STEPS: What you do**

#### UNDERMINING THE ROMANTIC RELATIONSHIP
LIST FIVE THINGS A NEWLY MARRIED FEMALE CAN DO TO
UNDERMINE HER RELATIONSHIP WITH A MALE.

1.

2.

3.

4.

5.

## AVOIDING DIFFICULTIES IN A RELATIONSHIP WITH YOUNG MEN

LIST FIVE WAYS A NEWLY MARRIED FEMALE CAN AVOID HAVING DIFFICULTIES IN A RELATIONSHIP WITH A YOUNG MAN.

1.

2.

3.

4.

5.

### Exercise 7.5
### HOW CAN YOU CHERISH HIM?

**Girlhood to Ladyhood**

**Dignity**:
Your responsibility to males

It is your responsibility as a female to treat ALL men with respect and vice versa. This means no name-calling, insults, hitting or violence of any kind—EVER! You have an obligation to keep from calling males profane names or using insulting remarks towards them. Your responsibility as a young lady is to support young men and women at all times regardless of how much you think they may provoke or mistreat you. *YOU ALWAYS HAVE A CHOICE!*

It is your responsibility to nurture a positive and healthy relationship with your partner. Whenever you can, anticipate his needs before he has a chance to express them. Under no circumstances is it ever appropriate for you to hit your mate, even if he threatens you. In some cases, hitting your mate is like trying to beat up a child who is much smaller than you. (Some females are actually larger and stronger than their boyfriends, for example.) It's an uneven match, and it is inexcusable. When a relationship is so out of control that it becomes violent, it is automatically no longer a genuine and healthy relationship. You should know you may be moving toward a physical conflict when you begin to have frequent arguments and verbal conflicts. It is your responsibility to try and talk through conflict peacefully or seek professional counseling if you cannot work out misunderstandings.

You have control over your behavior. You can choose to hit or not hit a young man. If he starts the mistreatment first with insults or hitting, let him know that this is *totally unacceptable* or seek out help to protect yourself! Work out an understanding when you first begin dating that neither of you will mistreat the other person in your relationship—no mistreatment by using insulting words or hurtful actions, like hitting, pushing, etc. SEEK PROFESSIONAL HELP FROM A SCHOOL, COMMUNITY COUNSELOR OR OTHER QUALIFIED PROFESSIONAL WHEN YOU ARE HAVING A HARD TIME HANDLING THIS KIND OF SITUATION ON YOUR OWN.

You can choose to curse or not curse a male. Decide that nothing a young man will do can **MAKE** you so angry that you have to try and hurt him because you are a lady. You hold yourself to a higher standard. It is all up to you. You MUST exercise self-control at all times in romantic relationships. An investment in your mate is an investment in yourself.

**Turning Girls into Ladies**

**A Multicultural, Behavioral Approach**
**Motherhood**

**Lesson 8**

Turning Girls into Ladies

A Multicultural, Behavioral Approach
Motherhood

Lesson 8

## LEARNING OBJECTIVES

**You should learn:**
- What it takes to be a mother.
- What the mother-child relationship should look like.
- The various roles of a mother.

**Exercise 8.1**
**Learning to Be a Mother**

**Girlhood to Womanhood PASSAGE**
Motherhood: Parent's Responsibility

A mother is far more than just a biological parent. She is a co-leader with her mate. They both are responsible for their child's full development. When a lady bears a child, she becomes responsible for providing the best care possible throughout her child's developing years. A lady shows maturity in exceeding the standards of caring for her child, whenever possible, sometimes meaning that she must sacrifice her personal needs and wants for the sake of the child.

Some young ladies may not have had the privilege of having caring parents who showed them love, affection, and commitment. Some young ladies may, therefore, as a result, become reluctant or simply do not know how to show genuine caring for their children. In these cases, the mother can benefit from training in ways to exercise well-tested positive influence methods of child-rearing and behavior management. Getting training in these methods can help the young lady to rise above what she may have missed in her relationship with her parents. Real ladies must be determined to end a cycle of ineffective parenting among families by developing a solid parenting skill set and using this training to step up to the motherhood challenge.

Great mothers focus on the child's changing needs as the child grows. Outstanding mothers set her own self-centeredness, criticism for the child, and a reluctance to be kind and understanding to her children aside. Model mothers are consistent in disciplining their children. These mothers exercise leadership by showing discipline in love, not anger. She takes time to understand each child's unique interests, mannerisms, and gifts. Her goal is to promote a whole and well-developed child and a family full of healthy relationships. The mature mother spends time with her children and expresses care and love to them through words and actions. The committed mother actively looks for opportunities to praise the positive things their children do while teaching and training where the children need help. What are some things a mother can do to form a close relationship with her child?

List three ways a mother can be a role model for her mate and family?

## Exercise 8.2

**The Mother's Parenting Lessons**
**WHO TRAINS THE CHILD?**
ANSWER THE FOLLOWING QUESTIONS BASED ON THE PRECEEDING PASSAGE

1. How does a girl usually learn what things she has to do to become a lady?

2. Who teaches her these lessons?

3. Who teaches a girl the most important lessons she needs to know in order to become a well-respected lady?

4. What would you, as a mother, need to do to teach a girl to become a lady?

## Exercise 8.3

**Mother-Daughter ROLE PLAY**

*STEPS: WHAT YOU DO*

*Participants will role-play the following scenario. Before beginning, the group should suggest 5 keywords from the training that a mother can use in her discussion with her son.*

Scenario

     A mother is trying to persuade her 16-year-old daughter to change her mean and ruthless behavior toward other people. The mother is very concerned with the direction in which her daughter's life is heading. The daughter is disrespectful toward adults at home and school and has been getting into constant fights with her brothers and sister.

USE THIS ROLE PLAY EXERCISE TO DEMONSTRATE TWO DIFFERENT WAYS FOR THE MOTHER IN THIS SITUATION TO ENCOURAGE HER DAUGHTER TO BE MORE RESPECTFUL TO PEOPLE AT HOME.

REPEAT THIS EXERCISE BUT SHOW THE WAY THAT THE MOTHER CAN TAILOR WHAT SHE SAYS TO HER DAUGHTER TO FIT WHAT GOES ON WITH HER DAUGHTER AT SCHOOL BETWEEN THE DAUGHTER AND TEACHERS, THE PRINCIPAL, THE COACH, ETC.

**SOLUTIONS**

     One answer to this problem is for the mother to start early in the young lady's life by encouraging her to see how treating people with respect, kindness, and thoughtfulness works in her favor in the long run. The mother's role is to give to the young lady words of credit where credit is due. She does this by telling her very clearly what actions and activities help him to grow as a man. The key is for the mother to be consistent and specific in supporting and encouraging the young lady to become a decent, well-rounded individual. Ideally the mother monitors the young lady's growth and helps to direct her toward becoming a leader, role model, and contributor to the community's well-being and success.

---

**Exercise 8.4**
**Mother-Daughter Role Play: LESSONS LEARNED**

**THE MOTHER'S LESSONS**

ANSWER THE FOLLOWING QUESTIONS BASED ON THE PRECEEDING PASSAGE

1.   What lessons did the daughter in the role play learn from the mother's discussion?

2.   If you were in the daughter's situation, how would you apply the mother's lessons?

---

**Exercise 8.5**

**The Mother's LEADERSHIP**

**Girlhood to Becoming a Lady PASSAGE**

**Motherhood Leaders: Many Roles**

The role of the mother, according to this leadership training, requires that the mother looks out for the overall well-being of her mate, children, and other immediate family members when needed. The mother can serve many roles such as breadwinner, protector, nurturer, and organizer. The mother and her intimate partner may agree to share some household responsibilities. Mothers can perform roles such as changing diapers, cooking, and cleaning, and that is fine if both parties agree on it. On the other hand, the lady of the house may choose to perform tasks like cutting the grass and washing the car. It is her choice, and she has the right to make that choice.

The main point is that in determining the most appropriate roles for the mother, the overall needs of the family must take a high priority. Family members must be satisfied with these varied and sometimes nontraditional roles for the family team to run smoothly. Mothers may or may not have the last word in making a decision. If the problem that a family is facing goes beyond the mother's knowledge or available time and resources to solve the problem, then she may need to get help from her friend, a professional, intimate partner, or mate. In a family that works well together, the mother and mate will be in agreement as to who performs what role in a healthy relationship.

All families are not the same. Some are single-parent families. Others are extended families with grandparents, aunts, and uncles, or even friends of the family who act as if they are biological family members. The key is that the best mothers who are leaders are responsible, unselfish, and dedicated to promoting the growth and success of their families. Mothers are not "friends" in the traditional family, but like a friend, great mothers will never lead you to danger or interfere with your success. They keep you safe and promote your success. This is your role as a mature lady in the 21st Century.

### Exercise 8.5 (Continued)
### The Mother's LEADERSHIP

### Girlhood to Lady Status PASSAGE

### Motherhood Leaders:  Many Roles

Write down your opinion about the main roles a mother can play in helping her family to become better and well-adjusted people who work together as a team. What, in your opinion, is the best way to make this happen?

**Turning Girls into Ladies**
**A Multicultural, Behavioral Approach**

**Ladies and Mass Media**

**Lesson 9**

**Making Sense of Music, Television, Videos, and Print Materials**

**Turning Girls into Ladies
A Multicultural, Behavioral Approach**

**Ladyhood and Mass Media**

**Making Sense of Music, Television, Videos, and Print Materials**

**Lesson 9**

**LEARNING OBJECTIVES**

**You Should Learn:**

- **How to judge whether a mass media message is beneficial**
- **What the hidden motives of media producers may be**
- **How to determine whether content producers have your interest at heart**

**Exercise 9.1**

**Role Play: Understanding How the Media Works - "Money Bags, Inc."**

**Girlhood to Womanhood for Ladies PASSAGE**

> **What does the term "mass media" mean?**
>
> **Answer: The term "mass media" refers to communication methods that reach large numbers of people to inform or entertain them. Mass media includes television, radio, newspapers, magazines, CDs recordings, and the Internet.**

**Mass Media and Ladyhood
Your Image and Influence**

Mass media can have a powerful effect on a young lady's self-image and influence because of the quality of what she consumes. This section will help you learn ways to make good judgments about the mass media that you see, hear, and read. You will also learn that the way you respond or the expression of your womanhood to the world around you is strongly influenced by mass media. Mass media impacts your self-view. Your self-view determines whether you see yourself positively or negatively. Mass media also influences the way you relate to people in your home, school, and neighborhood. The images that you see on television, hear on the radio, and read in publications can influence the amount of risk that you decide to take with people outside of your day-to-day encounters.

Mass media, in other words, entertainment products, are created because of a strong motivation for people who create them to earn money to live. There is nothing wrong with creating wholesome entertainment products. The problem is that some entertainment products can be detrimental to your mental and physical well-being. Often the entertainment creator's goal is to make the greatest achievable amount of money possible. This can be acceptable or unacceptable depending on the way the content of these products affects people's lives. It is the audience's responsibility to decide whether or not to buy it. Never forget that the point of the "Entertainment Business" is to make money for the individuals who create, produce, or package the entertainment. The reason a company usually chooses an idea for an entertainment product is that the project has the potential for yielding large profits. Once it becomes clear that a type of music, T.V. show, or magazine can generate high sales, the creators may turn out more and more products that are similar to each other.

* **To what degree do you think this passage is correct?  * Why do you agree or disagree?**

**Influencing the Audience**

For the mass media to make money, they must have an audience. For instance, companies recognize that they can draw large audiences to watch movies and listen to songs that have themes about today's ways of life. Company decision-makers recognize that some urban youth can identify with a "thug," "gangster," or "street-oriented" lifestyles, and the decision-makers use the young people's attraction to these lifestyles to get the young people to buy their products. Many young people today, urban or rural, adopt an urban lifestyle even though they have never really been personally exposed to that way of life. In the case of the music, the beat is what often draws young people to the music. It is also important to recognize the fact that many young people like this form of contemporary music, and they enjoy watching movies about glamorous and adventurous lifestyles. Therefore, they go to movies or listen to music that glorifies these lifestyles.

In recent years, we have seen a large number of songs that seem to focus on rebellious lifestyles and a substantial number of movies and reality shows that seem to make fighting, drug use, and mistreatment of each other acceptable. This acceptance of misbehavior did not occur by accident. It is arguably designed to increase the number of paying customers. Again, people who produce these songs and shows do it because it makes money for them.

There is nothing wrong with companies that make money from distributing entertainment products that target young people. Young people must understand, however, that sometimes making money is more important to companies than the unhealthy messages that their products convey. Some company representatives may make excuses for their products by saying that they are "just entertainment" regardless of whether they encourage harmful behavior. REMEMBER, IT'S SHOW ***BUSINESS***! Therefore, young people have to learn how to look out for their own interests on the occasions when people in the media try to take advantage of them for money.

| CREATED TO MAKE COMPANIES MONEY: "SHOW BUSINESS" |
| --- |
| ONCE IT BECOMES CLEAR THAT A SELECTED TYPE OF MUSIC, T.V. SHOW, OR WRITTEN FORM OF ENTERTAINMENT CAN GENERATE HIGH SALES, COMPANIES AND THE PRODUCERS WHO WORK ON THESE PROJECTS WANT TO MAKE MORE AND MORE OFF THESE PRODUCTS.  IN THIS WAY, THEY CAN MAKE MORE MONEY.  SADLY SOME PEOPLE MAY CARE MORE ABOUT THE MONEY THAN THEY CARE ABOUT YOU! |

### Examine the Creative Process

Just about every television show or movie that you see starts as a book. For a movie, this book is called a *script*, not to different in purpose from this workbook. The book describes everything that a film producer will need to consider in order to make a movie or television show. Many times this book, or script, goes through several extensive rewrites before the person who is making the movie is ready to begin making the motion picture or it is digitally recorded. The writers may change the characters' names, the story ending, or completely change the setting where the movie takes place if they think the change will generate larger audiences and make more money. For example, in some cases, amazingly, you can make $100,000 from the sale of a single script.  This is not unusual in Hollywood.

This is why reading and writing are so very important to making a living in the television and movie industry. People in the television industry need talented workers who can read and write very well. They need people who can create an original idea that is interesting enough for people to want to see the product in a theater, on television, or rented online.

Companies want people who can create good, original ideas for songs that will sell large numbers of recordings. The quality of their work has to be appealing enough to sell to young people across the country. Many hours of planning go into making the movies we see and music we hear on a national and international level. This is the reason why music producers often carefully focus on the beat in a song because they know this is what young people will purchase.

There is nothing automatically wrong with rap music by itself. There is nothing necessarily wrong with television shows and movies about criminal lifestyles, for example, by themselves. Remember that anyone who creates music, books, newspapers and other forms of entertainment do so to make money. The question is, "Does the artist look out for the health, safety and success of his or her audience when making music, videos, books, magazines and computer games?" The quality of the content of some artists' work shows they care a lot about their fans. In other cases, the artist's content has little redeeming value in their work that contributes to the fan's health or success. When the artist does not appear to care about what happens to the fans, the fan herself must be responsible for herself. Many personal and social problems may occur for young people when the artist's ONLY concern is putting together creative works that sell. Many people believe that placing curse words, violence and criminal activity in music, television and music videos can have a harmful effect on young people. Placing corrupt information in mass media content can make young people numb to other people's misery.

## Is the Artist a Friend to their Fans?

Young people looking for mass media products or entertainment should apply the definition for what makes a friend. ***Remember, a friend is someone who will never lead you into danger or interfere with your success.*** Similarly, if an actor, singer, musician, writer, or company spokesperson attempts to sell you unhealthy ideas and images, "THEY ARE NOT YOUR FRIEND!" It is important to be able to tell the difference between healthy and degrading entertainment. It is equally critical that you allow only healthy entertainment to enter your mind as it is to allow only wholesome food to enter your body. Is it acceptable to consume rotten entertainment any more than eating foul, decayed food? WHAT DO YOU THINK?

## YOUR Success vs. Mass Media Profit

- Most visual art forms like plays, movies, or other television shows begin as a book or script.

- Great writing and reading skills are essential for telling a story through music, videos, movies, or television shows.

Ask yourself, "Is the music artist, movie actor, music video maker, or recording company your friend?" **Remember, a friend is someone who will never lead you to danger or interfere with your success!**

## Exercise 9.2
## Role Play: Understanding How the Media Works – "Money Bags Productions, Inc."

**STEPS: What you do**

Situation One: Have the participants role-play the following scenario. Encourage them to find a solution that protects young people who will be buying this product.

Several people are sitting around a conference table creating a new music video aimed at entertaining young people in the 13 to 15-year-old age group. Mr. Bob Yougotta Ripemoff, the President of the company, is instructing his Creative Team to be sure the music video has the "right stuff" to generate at least $175,000 in profits for the company in the first month of its nationwide release.

**Cast of Characters:**
1. Company President: Mr. Bob Yougotta Ripemoff
2. Music Artist and Vocalist: Ghetto Blade
3. Company Marketing Representative: Wanda Wooden-Nickel
4. Video Producer: Thadeus Thuglife

**Scenario One:**
Money Bags Productions, Inc.

President Mr. Bob Yougotta Ripemoff is upset that the company has not made a profit in the last six months. The company has been unable to generate hits from the artists who made it famous. The company recently signed a contract, however, with a young man named Ghetto Blade, a vocalist who has a surprise hit that is very different from Money Bags' style.

Mr. Ripemoff wants his video producer to make a video for Ghetto Blade's song that has cursing (full of the B _ _ _ _ word), gang-related activity, and sexual references added to the song's lyrics. He says he could care less about who could catch HIV by being influenced to participate in unsafe, risky sexual behavior. He says, "It's their problem if they die from being so stupid." Mr. Ripemoff has made it very clear that anyone who does not go along with his program will be fired immediately.

Vocalist, Ghetto Blade, is strongly resisting the idea of distributing music that could be harmful to young people. Ghetto Blade wants to create a music video that encourages young people not to drink alcohol, use illegal drugs or engage in risky sexual behavior. He wants his fans to practice brotherhood and promote harmony among young people.

Company Marketing Representative, Wanda Wooden-Nickel, refers to a study that proves using cursing and female dancers in bikinis in videos will help the playlist to generate $225,000 in the first month of release. She says the 13 to 15-year-old market alone has enough money and desire to purchase this type of music. Wooden-Nickel says the music has the right urban beat, and with some hardcore rap mixed with Ghetto Blade's vocals, it would skyrocket. Ghetto Blade says he will do everything in his power to keep from making the violent music video containing anything that will degrade young people.

Mr. Ripemoff says he will not stand for any disagreement on the part of any artist. Mr. Ripemoff says he doesn't even need Ghetto Blade in the video.
Video Producer, Thadeus Thuglife, is not very happy about the requirements the President is requesting but decides to go along with the President's wishes in order to save his job. Ghetto Blade realizes the three executives in the room outnumber him, and the staff continues to plan the video. They include unfavorable comments using cursing, drugs, and gang activity in the music video. They decide to do so even though Ghetto Blade wants to take a stand for what he thinks is right. After all, the contract gives them that authority.

### Exercise 9.3
### More Role Play: Understanding How the Media Works  - "Money Bags Productions, Inc." STEPS: What you do

**Situation Two**: Prepare a one-person role play using the following scenario.

In this role play, your job is to teach ways to make good decisions about what kind of music to listen to. This time, Money Bags Productions, Inc. has already released the playlist and music video mentioned in the previous story. The CD is full of foul language, sexual gestures and violent expressions. The company is conducting special promotions in inner-city entertainment locations. Money Bags Productions Inc. is making a tremendous amount of money from the products. Some young people who listen to the music wanted to purchase it so badly that they made up stories to get money from their parents. There are television reports that young people across the country are imitating the music video's extreme violence. Several young people died as a result of imitating the stories depicted in the music.

In the role play, persuade your fellow participants to understand that they are being abused by Money Bags Productions, Inc. Make them understand that listening to popular music is generally not a problem. It is a problem, however, to take advantage of young people by presenting harmful images simply to get their money. ***Include the definition for a friend in your argument against harmful music. (Definition:  A friend will never lead you to danger or interfere with your success.)*** Explain to the participants that they can choose to turn off music and not buy it as a commitment to their own healthy lifestyle rather than giving into a temporarily appealing, but harmful fad.
**STEPS: What you do**

**Situation III:**

      In this role play, Ghetto Blade successfully convinces the company to make a healthy video that young people can purchase. Four participants will role-play the Money Bags Productions, Inc. characters Company President Mr. Bob Yougotta Ripemoff, Musical Artist and Vocalist Ghetto Blade, Company Marketing Representative Wanda Wooden-Nickel, and Video Producer, Thadeus Thuglife in the Conference Room discussing a workable plan for making $175,000 from the sale of the playlist and music video in the product's first-month release. This time, vocalist Ghetto Blade takes control and demands that a positive product be made. He outlines elements that will be appealing to young people across the country. Each one of the other characters at first remains convinced about their individual beliefs regarding the creation of the music video. In other words, they must strongly state their position on making the negative video. Ghetto Blade, however, has compelling examples of playlists and music videos that have made money with positive elements in them. In the end, because Ghetto Blade stood his ground, even when he could have lost his contract, he wins his position because the company is looking for ways to make profits. Ghetto Blade becomes a billionaire because he stood his ground!

---

### YOU JUDGE THE ENTERTAINMENT PRODUCT!

**PEOPLE WHO MAKE THESE T.V., MUSIC VIDEOS, ETC. MAY NOT BE YOUR FRIENDS. THEY MAY LIKE MAKING MONEY MORE THAN THEY CARE ABOUT YOU! LEARN TO MAKE YOUR OWN JUDGEMENTS. DO SEX, DRUGS, AND VIOLENCE FIT WITH BECOMING A MATURE LADY WHO IS A REAL LEADER?**

---

**HARMFUL PLAYLIST**

LIST SOME MUSIC TITLES YOU HAVE HEARD RECENTLY THAT INFLUENCE YOUNG PEOPLE IN A NEGATIVE WAY.

     1.

     2.

     3.

     4.

     6.

7.

8.

9.

10.

11.

In what ways is this list likely to cause young people to make bad choices in their lives?

How can negative lyrics in music influence alcohol and drug use?

How can negative music encourage young people to participate in unprotected sex and POSSIBLY contract HIV?

**GOOD PLAYLIST**

LIST SOME MUSIC TITLES YOU HAVE HEARD RECENTLY THAT INFLUENCE YOUNG PEOPLE IN A POSITIVE WAY.

1.

2.

3.

4.

6.

7.

8.

9.

10.

| Which is the more persuasive playlist?<br>Which PLAYLIST IS LONGER OR TOOK THE LEAST TIME TO COMPLETE? |
| --- |
| Circle one:  Positive or Negative<br>Explain why you believe this playlist is more or less persuasive. |
|  |
|  |
|  |
|  |
|  |
|  |

**Turning Girls into Ladies**

**A Multicultural, Behavioral Approach**

**How to Handle People**

**Who Treat You Unfairly**

**Lesson 10**

# Turning Girls into Ladies
## A Multicultural, Behavioral Approach

### How to Handle People Who Treat You Unfairly

### Lesson 10

## LEARNING OBJECTIVE
## You should learn:

- Ways to respond to people who make negative judgments about young ladies simply because they are young females.
- Ways to cope with mistreatment caused by racial, ethnic, or other bias.
- Healthy ways to respond to members of other racial and ethnic groups when the young lady interprets their actions as disrespectful.

## Exercise 10.1
## How to Handle People Who Mistreat You

Too often, females must learn to deal with the reality that some people in our society view them with suspicion, fear, and mistrust simply because they are young females. Individuals exhibiting this behavior may be Caucasian, Asian, Latino-Hispanic, or other females. The common thread tying these individuals together is the fact that they all hold unfavorable opinions of young females. Their reasons may be diverse and personal experiences with a few young females, negative images from mass media or messages they have picked up from others in society.

It is a sensitive issue for individuals who maintain judgmental beliefs and behaviors toward young ladies. It is just as sensitive to the young women who are unfairly judged before they have a chance to prove themselves otherwise. People who hold negative attitudes toward young females view them as having identical morals and values even though young ladies are very different from each other. It is especially problematic at the public level and many times in private places in society as young ladies come face to face with their accusers. These are emotionally high-risk interactions for the accusers and girls. For young females, historically, the damage from false accusations to their self-concept or self-image may increase over their lifespan. When the accusations are true, they may often lead to more severe labeling by others in society. A small number of young females may see these encounters as assaults on their femininity and a possible desire to retaliate. Being the object of stereotyping for too many young women is an unpleasant attack on their basically good character. In an excessive number of cases when this occurs, these events are considered mental assaults that have far-reaching consequences.

**Learn to Overcome Stereotyping**

Let us examine ways to handle being judged unfairly in public places like school, government offices, stores, restaurants, family conflicts, and so on, no matter who you are. The good news is that you can learn to rise above mistreatment and thrive if you smartly handle each situation.

Young women can learn to cultivate a mature approach to handling people who treat them unfairly. One way is to learn to recognize unfairness and injustice. It is important to recognize real conditions where injustice happens because of who you are. It is essential that you learn to make healthy and effective responses to these situations. This is because handling mistreatment correctly can keep you from being suspended from school, out of jail and other bad outcomes. At the same time, it is wise to avoid being too sensitive to mistreatment. Sometimes a young female is the object of maltreatment because the other person has not been taught how to treat all people fairly. The mistreatment is not always racially motivated or because of gender. It is worthwhile to use good judgment in handling these situations regardless of the reason for the mistreatment.

Learning to respond effectively to these situations serves the best interests of the young male. It is your responsibility to overcome desires to become hostile in response to an improper aggressor. Likewise, young ladies have to learn not to let mistreatment from others get under their skin in a way that, in the long run, can contribute to unhealthy stress reactions, high blood pressure, strokes and heart attacks. These harmful internal reactions can add up over a period of time and take a toll on how long a person lives. Some young women feel that because of who they are, they do not have access to the same resources that others do to approach life's challenges and succeed. It is critical for young women to learn ways to adapt satisfactorily to feelings of mistreatment. You can learn to become a well-rounded, mature lady who responds to mistreatment in a smart way, and you come out the winner in the long run. Making this adjustment is essential whenever genuine mistreatment occurs.

**Sometimes it is Just a Misunderstanding**

Often young women find themselves in uncomfortable and possibly dangerous circumstances for whatever reason. For one, some young ladies do not know how to respond appropriately or are too quick to respond to a situation of possible mistreatment in ways that make the situation worse. Some fail to step back from the situation and examine it clearly. Failure to keep a cool head can place young women and others at risk. This can involve a public situation, a couple's relationship, or a family conflict. The situation often results from misunderstanding or unclear communication. For people who are quick to respond with anger, insults, and violence, their aggressive behavior can result in jail time, injury, or death. The next two sets of exercises teach young ladies alternative ways to cope with actual mistreatment when these harmful actions are based on the young woman's skin color, personality, life choices or cultural group. In these exercises, you will experiment with making adjustments to specific situations that they may encounter in their day-to-day interactions with others.

**Exercise 10.1**
**Identifying Examples of Mistreatment in Your Life**
HAS THERE EVER BEEN A TIME WHEN SOMEONE UNFAIRLY JUDGED YOU BECAUSE OF WHO YOU ARE? EXAMPLES: AGE, WEIGHT, CULTURE, INCOME, ETC. HOW DID THAT MAKE YOU FEEL?

LIST SOME EFFECTIVE WAYS TO HANDLE SITUATIONS LIKE THIS.

**Exercise 10.2**
**Handling People Who Treat You Unfairly**

1.  How could you become trapped into holding on to past negative experiences dealing with people who do not seem to trust you because of who you are?

2.  Why should a young lady learn new ways to respond to what other people say about her even if it is not wrong?

3.  In the areas listed below, what can a young lady do to be the best person that she can be?

    Communications

    Education

    Relationships

    Public Image

4.  How would you, as a young lady, explain your culture (music, dress, speech) to a person from another culture who says, "I don't get it?"

**Exercise 10.3**
**Communicating and Working with People Who May Not Understand Your Culture**

**STEPS: What You Do**

The following exercises recognize that a critical part of becoming a mature lady in the future will be to understand that the world is getting smaller. This means that it is more and more likely that you will need to work with other people for your benefit and theirs. People from all over the world come in contact and communicate with each other more often because of air travel, videoconferencing and so on. Events that occur on one side of the globe can have an immediate effect on a location on the other side of the world. People can learn what happens more quickly and travel to other countries more easily. The ways we were used to relating to each other may not be effective now and in the future. It is important to learn to cooperate with other cultural and ethnic groups for the success you may be seeking. Successful young ladies from all backgrounds must learn to get along well with all types of people regardless of whether they are Caucasian, Latino-Hispanic, Asian or otherwise. It is critical for young ladies to find ways to avoid carrying distrust, blame, or ill feelings against any group.

| COMMUNICATING WITH OTHER CULTURAL GROUPS OF PEOPLE WHY WOULD YOU BE MORE LIKELY TO SUCCEED IF YOU BECOME BETTER ABLE TO COMMUNICATE WITH PEOPLE FROM OTHER RACES AND CULTURES? EXPLAIN. |
| --- |
|  |
|  |
|  |
|  |
|  |

**WORKING WITH OTHER CULTURAL BACKGROUNDS**
WHAT ARE SOME STEPS YOU COULD TAKE TO WORK
SMOOTHLY WITH PEOPLE FROM OTHER INCOME LEVELS,
GENDERS, RACES, AND CULTURES?

1.

2.

3.

4.

5.

6.

7.

8.

9.

10.

# Turning Girls into Ladies

## A Multicultural, Behavioral Approach

## How to Deal with Authorities

## Lesson 11

# Turning Girls into Ladies

## A Multicultural, Behavioral Approach

## How to Deal with Authorities

## Lesson 11

**LEARNING OBJECTIVES**
**YOU SHOULD LEARN:**
- To display nonverbal examples of behaviors that allow you to respond appropriately to harassment from law enforcement and other officials.
- Learn ways to keep out of trouble with authorities.

**Exercise 11.1**
**Read this story.**

Your parents sent you to the county courthouse to pick up some business papers. You and your friend, Danielle, have never been there before. When you entered the courthouse, you placed your belongings on a conveyor sending them through the X-ray machine. You both proceeded through the metal detector, and the officer frisked and scanned you with his hand-held detector. You asked the officer, "Where is the clerk's office?" The officer pointed to the courthouse directory down the hall. The directory showed the Clerk's Office is in Room 508. You and Danielle walked to the elevator and pushed the up button, which lit up.

While waiting, a young lady walked up. She looked at you, rolled her eyes and pressed the up button, which was already lit as though you did not know you needed to press the elevator button. The elevator arrived and the door opened. Looking at the two of you, an older lady inside the elevator, very afraid, said, "Oh, my God!" and moved quickly past you as though she thought you were going to attack her. You and Danielle got on the elevator behind the first lady. You pushed the button for the 5th Floor. She pushed the button for the 9th floor, then looked at the two of you and clutched her purse tightly. Insulted by this series of events, you wanted to say something mean. After leaving the Clerk's Office, you and Danielle discussed ways you could have responded to the officer's lack of assistance and the two ladies' obvious distrust of the two of you.

| PEOPLE WHO FEAR YOU IN ISOLATED PLACES DESCRIBE HOW YOU WOULD HANDLE SITUATIONS ON ELEVATORS OR IN OTHER ISOLATED PLACES WHERE SOME PEOPLE MAY VERBALLY OR PHYSICALLY OBJECT TO YOUR PRESENCE. |
| --- |
|  |
|  |
|  |
|  |

**Exercise 11.2**
**Department Store Encounter**
**Read this story.**

Imagine that you are in a department store. You came to the store to purchase a skirt and scarf for a family member's wedding. You walked into the women's department and noticed a store clerk two isles away who is straightening packages of blouses. You picked up a couple of scarves to inspect but could not decide which of them you like better. You decided to take the two scarves to the lingerie section. While on your way, you noticed that another clerk had joined the first clerk. It is obvious that both clerks were watching your every move. You began to feel uncomfortable about the situation.

You decided that you will respond to their behavior. You asked the first clerk if he can help you match the two scarves you have selected with a couple of blouses. One of the clerks told you he has some blouses that would be perfect matches but said the items are probably too expensive for you. You were surprised about what he said.

After choosing the scarves and blouses that you think go well together, you quickly moved to the women's jewelry display. You looked for a pair of bracelets to complement the blouses. The clerk removed the jewelry from the display case for you. You examined the bracelets briefly and decided you would wear the bracelets you already have at home.

As you were telling the jewelry clerk you did not want the bracelets, you saw the previous two clerks still observing you. You walked to the clerks with the scarves and blouses in hand. You explained that you were planning to make a jewelry purchase and asked why were they observing you so closely? One of them said, "Do you want these scarves and blouses or not? We get a lot of people in this store like you acting as if they intend to buy the whole store and then the merchandise goes missing in action."

You handed over your department store credit card to the clerk. She asked for your identification, processed the account number for payment, and the cash register approved your transaction. The clerk checked closely to compare your signature on the credit card with your identification signature.

**SOLUTIONS: What are some appropriate ways to deal with this situation?**
- **Ask to speak to the store manager.**
- **Write a letter of concern to the corporate office.**
- **Register your concern with the Better Business Bureau (BBB).**
- **Ask your parents to call to speak to company officials on your behalf.**
- **Always be polite and civil. You can be assertive without being disrespectful.**

**Exercise 11.3**
**Handling POLICE HARASSMENT**

**Read this story**

You were riding down the street in a wealthy part of town. You were on your way home after leaving a co-worker's house. One of your parents is an attorney, and the other is an architect. You were driving a late model nice car. Your coworker, Erica, gave you free concert tickets she could not use because she had a family emergency out of town. You had to pick up the tickets that night because Erica planned to leave town that morning at 6:00 a.m. Returning home through the upscale neighborhood, you noticed a lot of people eating and drinking outside at some street-level, open-air restaurants. Many of the customers at these establishments appeared intoxicated, and they made gestures to encourage you to join them. You were fascinated with the scene; so, you slowed down to see whether they were serious. Just as you looked up into your rear-view mirror, you heard a siren and saw flashing blue lights. It took a minute or so for you to recognize that this police car was trying to pull you over to the side of the road. You pulled over, and the officer asked whether your automobile insurance was current, knowing that it showed active in the police database.

The police officer asked you to show him your driver's license, registration, and proof of insurance. You showed him the license in the see-through compartment of your wallet, and he asked you to take the license out of the plastic compartment of the wallet. You began searching through the glove compartment for your insurance card when the police officer asked you to get out of the car.

"Spread 'em!" he said as he pushed you onto your car and began to search you for weapons or illegal items. You tried to explain that you were headed home after picking up some tickets from a coworker. You asked the officer, "What do you want from me? Do I look like a criminal or something?" With an insulting and harsh tone, the officer responded saying, "Now that you mention it, you do look like a suspect who robbed the grocery store a few blocks away this morning?" The suspect may have been driving a car like this one. The people at the restaurant were looking at you as if you were a criminal, and you were embarrassed.

Every time you tried to explain yourself, the officer said, "Turn around and shut up." By this time, the officer's partner had run a computer check for a stolen car and any outstanding warrants that you might have. The car was not stolen, and there was no reason to interrupt you from continuing your ride across town. The only hitch was that the officer still wanted to see your proof of insurance and threatened to write you a ticket. You stated that the insurance card was somewhere in the glove compartment. You reminded him that if you did not have insurance, the police computer would have indicated it when his partner ran your license.

After looking around for a few minutes, you found the insurance card and tried to give it to the officer. He snatched it out of your hand and said, "You spoiled brats are all alike." He looked at it and verified that your insurance was current. He said to you, "Sorry for the delay, but the next time have your insurance card ready, rich girl." You drove off feeling mistreated and disrespected but recognized the situation could have been much worse.

**What should you do next? Which of the following are the best options?**
- Get the officer's badge number and name off of his uniform. Call his supervisor to explain your concerns. Follow up in writing with a letter.
- Send an email to his supervisor and describe what happened in detail. Attach photos and videos if you can.
- Make an appointment with the police community relations department to express your concerns.
- Remain respectful to the officer at the time of the incident. Follow his directions and go on about your business as quickly as possible.

## TIPS FOR DEALING WITH POLICE
## HOW TO TAKE CONTROL
## BEING THE SMART ONE IN THE SITUATION

- Remember that all police officers are not bad regardless of their background or culture

- Refer to the officer with respect by calling her or him "officer," "ma'am," or "sir," for examples.

- At all costs, avoid cursing at the officer.

- Be as polite and respectable as possible.

- Say, "Is there anything that I can do for you, officer?" Show the officer your license, etc.

- Keep your hands visible.

- Follow the officer's directions.

- Remember that it is better to have hurt feelings than a physical injury or face being jailed unnecessarily.

- Give him the benefit of the doubt.

- Assume that the officer is trying to do his or her job.

- Think to yourself, "Oh, he's only doing his job. I'll just give him what he wants."

- Always respond to the situation in a legal and civil manner on the next day or a time after you have completely left the situation. Recording the incident at the time may be appropriate as long as your approach is legal. Never curse or use insulting language.

- Note: By being respectful and making good choices, you can decrease the chance of turning a routine stop into a conflict or perhaps time in jail. You do not have to act like a coward to be respectful.

- Many of the honest officers are just trying to do their jobs as well as they can.

**Turning Girls into Ladies**
**A Multicultural, Behavioral Approach**

**Learning to Prevent Violence,**

**Manage Conflict, and Select Real Friends**

**Lesson 12**

**Turning Girls into Ladies**
**A Multicultural, Behavioral Approach**

**Learning to Prevent Violence,**

**Manage Conflict, and Select Real Friends**

**Lesson 12**

## LEARNING OBJECTIVES
You should learn to:

- Discuss ways that conflict affects the way people like you live and ways you can thrive.
- Give examples of conflict and how it starts between people.
- List ways to help friends and other young people prevent and manage conflict in a healthy way.
- Learn two ways to tell whether "a running partner" or associate is really your friend.

## Exercise 12.1
CONFLICT: STOPPING IT BEFORE IT STARTS AND KEEPING IT FROM HAPPENING

**STEPS: What you do**
Consider what these words mean: Conflict, Prevention, and Management.

- What is conflict?
- Give an example of a conflict:
  (Working definition: A verbal or physical clash or trouble between two or more people.)
- What is prevention?
- Give an example of prevention:
  Working definition: Keeping an event from occurring before it happens.)
  What is management (of conflict)?
- Give an example of management.

**Exercise 12.2**
**Types of Conflict**

**STEPS: What you do**
List 5 types of actions or behaviors that show that people are in conflict.

1.

2.

3.

4.

5.

**Exercise 12.3**
Preventing Conflict

**STEPS: What you do**
List 5 types of conflict that have been in the news lately.

1.

2.

3.

4.

5.

List two types of conflict you see at school or in your neighborhood.

1.

2.

Which do you see more: Conflict with words or physical attacks?

## Exercise 12.4

When Conflict starts to grow, STOP IT IN ITS TRACKS!

**STEPS: What you do**

Consider the following example of conflict and how it starts between two people.

Jane (to her friend): "You are an idiot."
Gina (feeling bad): "Who, me?"
Gina must now decide what to say or what action to take.

WAYS TO AVOID CONFLICT
CIRCLE WHICH OF THE FOLLOWING CHOICES YOU WOULD TAKE
IF YOU WERE GINA.
1. Call Jane a name.
2. Threaten to hurt Jane.
3. Say, "Oh, she didn't mean it."
4. Hit Jane.
5. Don't pay attention to Jane.
6. Leave the situation.

EXPLAIN YOUR CHOICE IN THE BLANK SPACES:

OTHER WAYS TO AVOID CONFLICT

HERE ARE SOME EXAMPLES OF HOW TO HANDLE CONFLICT IN
VARIOUS SITUATIONS:

Hang around people who do not like to cause conflict.
Stay away from places where trouble happens a lot.
Protect yourself by ignoring people who say mean things to you.
Practice self-control and ways not to let what other people say or do affect you in a bad way.
Keep track of your choices in your head.
Examine the different actions you could take and choose the safest way to conduct yourself.
Practice replacing bad thoughts about yourself with good thoughts every day: "I'm a fantastic person." (This can build confidence so you will not have to be pulled into conflict or part of the gang, for example.)

**Girlhood to Becoming a Mature Lady**

**When Friends Criticize**
**Learn to Enjoy Alone Time**

What should you do when friends criticize you? Often people take criticism and choose unhealthy relationships because they do not want to be alone. If someone criticizes you, you may want to spend more time with real, long-term friends. Some friends may not be as popular or cool as others, but they may be very good at encouraging you to meet your life goals. When you can't be with good friends, learn to enjoy being alone. Be comfortable spending time alone reading, studying, and working on a computer to invest in your future. Talk with your family about finding creative ways to occupy your time. Use time alone to master more successful skills that you don't have already.

In making new friends, think about whether they are people who you can depend on in an emergency? Would they visit or rescue you in the hospital or jail if an emergency occurred? In some close relationships, people want to be your friends for selfish purposes. They start by making you think that you are cool to get you to think you are part of their group. As long as you do what the new friend wants, she remains friendly.

When friends start criticizing you a lot, often it may be their weapon to try to control you. When you do not know a person's background, you could be asking for trouble by spending time with them. For instance, the person who encourages you to do things that could get you into trouble with the law may not be there to bail you out in a serious situation. This may be because if she goes to jail to visit you, the police officers may lock her in jail for something she has already done wrong. Whenever you get in trouble with the police, many times the first thing the person does is replace you. She finds someone else who is easy for her to control for her own benefit. This person may be happy to sacrifice your future to advance her own future, to build up her reputation, or just to use you for her entertainment. Her initial kindness and affection may simply be a way to take advantage of you.

These kinds of friends may be girls in grown women's bodies as we talked about in Lesson One. At times, although she is an adult in years, she may be too childlike to see that she is exposing you to danger or interfering with your success. In either case, you may wish to think twice about how important the person's opinion and friendship are to you. **REMEMBER: A FRIEND WILL NEVER LEAD YOU TO DANGER OR INTERFERE WITH YOUR SUCCESS!** When conflict occurs, remember that you do not have to let other people define who you are. You do not have to do what they want you to do just because you do not want to be alone. If they criticize you constantly, but they never encourage you, it is a sign to walk away from the relationship.

**STEPS: What you do**

List three consequences of choosing to stay away from popular friends who often get into trouble—especially when you really like to be around that person?

1.

2.

3.

## Exercise 12.6

Positive Affirmation GAME FOR YOUNG MEN

**STEPS: What you do**

- The facilitator will choose two teams. (The ideal number of players on each team is 3-5 for a total of 6-10 players in the game.)
- A member of each team takes turns making a statement describing the way she wants to see herself in five years. (Examples: Fill in the blanks for Table 12.A.)
- Each team member must choose a Positive Word to include in her statement from Table 12.A.
- Make the statement in the most AUDIBLE, BELIEVABLE, AND CONVINCING way possible!
- Each time a team member completes her turn, her team must show sisterhood by clapping for her. Clap enthusiastically for her positive statement no matter what she says.
- The facilitator will rate how well the team member delivers her positive affirmation statement and the level of support from her team.
    - Affirmation Statements—Quality Scores
        - Needs work = 0
        - Acceptable = 1
        - Good delivery = 2
        - Excellent = 3
    - Team Support for each other—Sisterhood Scores
        - Needs work = 0
        - Acceptable = 1
        - Good delivery = 2
        - Excellent = 3
- The team with the highest summary score after at least three rounds wins the affirmation competition.

**Preventing and Managing Conflict**
**TABLE 12.A**
**Sisterhood Development**

Positive Words

| Mature | Fabulous | Decent |
|---|---|---|
| Outstanding | Amazing | Strong |
| Awesome | Fantastic | Incredible |
| Respectful | Secure | Positive |
| Exceptional | Brave | Constructive |
| Spectacular | Excellent | Superb |
| Thoughtful | Considerate | Marvelous |

Fill in the blank with an appropriate word from the above list

1. I'm a _____ young woman.

2. I'm a _____ young lady because I consider.

3. Everyone knows that I am a _____ person who knows how to stay out of trouble because I know how to think for myself.

4. I'm a _____ young lady because I consider other people's feelings to stay out of trouble.

6. Knowing how to prevent conflict makes me a _____ young woman.

7. I try to avoid hurting other people in order to stay out of trouble and this makes me

_____.

8. I will use _____ to help avoid conflicts with peers.

| Affirmation Game Score Sheet | |
|---|---|
| Team A | Team B |
| **Round 1** | |
| Affirmation Statements—Quality Scores<br>Needs work = 0<br>Acceptable = 1<br>Good delivery = 2<br>Excellent = 3 | Affirmation Statements—Quality Scores<br>Needs work = 0<br>Acceptable = 1<br>Good delivery = 2<br>Excellent = 3 |
| Judge's rating of the affirmation _____ | Judge's rating of the affirmation _____ |
| Team Support for each other—Sisterhood Scores<br>Needs work = 0<br>Acceptable = 1<br>Good delivery = 2<br>Excellent = 3 | Team Support for each other—Sisterhood Scores<br>Needs work = 0<br>Acceptable = 1<br>Good delivery = 2<br>Excellent = 3 |
| Judge's rating of team support _____ | Judge's rating of team support _____ |
| **Round 2** | |
| Judge's rating of the affirmation _____ | Judge's rating of the affirmation _____ |
| Judge's rating of team support _____ | Judge's rating of team support _____ |
| **Round 3** | |
| Judge's rating of the affirmation _____ | Judge's rating of the affirmation _____ |
| Judge's rating of team support _____ | Judge's rating of team support _____ |
| **Round 4** | |
| Judge's rating of the affirmation _____ | Judge's rating of the affirmation _____ |
| Judge's rating of team support _____ | Judge's rating of team support _____ |

**Positive and Negative Points of MAKING NONVIOLENT CHOICES**

## GIRLHOOD TO BECOMING A LADY

### Preventing Conflict

One way to keep your friends and other young people your age out of verbal and physical conflicts is by staying out of their arguments and fights. In other words, refuse to go along with making the situation worse. Learn to accept other people for who they are. It's OK for people to be different from you. You don't have to try to make others act just like you to feel good about yourself. You can accept other people without accepting all of their actions.

When you master the ability to accept people for who they are, this means that you have become a smarter, stronger, and more mature person. ***This is how a mature woman thinks** **and acts: Accepting people even though they are different.*** You can be happy, and at the same time, you do not have to feel that you have to go along with the crowd.

Make a big impact in your life by becoming a street smart young lady. There is nothing wrong with being very concerned or possibly afraid under the right conditions. You do not have to get into conflict just to prove that you are a "woman" or a "tough girl." You do not have to "woman up," as they say, to prove that you are a "real" woman.

Remember that you can be a great person regardless of what people say about you. The way to do this is to show that you genuinely care for other people by putting yourself in their places. It all depends on the way that you choose to respond to situations. You can learn how to adjust to situations by performing some of the following actions. You can control your feelings and actions by making smart choices. Learn to be wise by seeking out experienced people with wisdom and character. When you learn to adjust well to bad situations, you become more flexible and more mature.

### A Mature Person Knows When to Listen to Someone Else

In scientific work like chemistry, there is a test that tells whether a liquid is harmless or harmful. A liquid can burn you if it is too much like acid or too much like alkaline. When you put a specially treated piece of paper (litmus paper) in a liquid, one type of this paper will turn blue if the liquid is too strong in one direction (alkaline). Another type of paper will turn pink to show whether the liquid is acidic. *This is called a litmus test.*

Imagine that you are giving a test to the young people around you who call themselves your friends. Some may fail the test because they are not really your friends. *A friend will never lead you to danger or interfere with your success.* In order to lead yourself in the correct direction, you must check out every friend to determine whether the person is helpful or harmful to your future—like a litmus test. Sometimes they can be harmful to your future without knowing that they are being harmful. The person may be misguided because of never having a sufficiently positive life-long influence.

Many times young women and men get into trouble because they don't take the time to figure out whether a person that they know is exposing them to something dangerous or encouraging them to do something that can be harmful. It is important to know how to perform a human litmus test to judge who is a friend and who is not. In some cases, a so-called friend may try to trick you into doing something unhealthy by making fun of you or implying that they do not want to be your friend. You can be the smart one in the situation by stepping back from the situation and taking a long hard look at who is influencing you in a way that steers you off your course to success.

Choosing violence to solve your problems can interfere with your success. Select friends who are smart enough to work out differences with people in a calm, peaceful manner. This is the way that a mature woman behaves. This is how a mature woman thinks and acts.

**What's Your Test of Friendship?**
What if the answer to the friendship litmus test is no, the person is not your friend? The person's opinion or false friendship will not help your educational, mental, social, spiritual, or financial standing in life. It won't help you to pay any bills or fulfill personal obligations now or in the future. The person is trying to get you to do something that you know is wrong, place you in danger, or keep you from being successful. You should strongly consider ignoring the person's opinion. The person's friendship or recognition may not be worth your time or effort in the long run. The person may be immature and undermine your path to a better life. It doesn't matter how they try to criticize you for not doing what they want you to do.

Sometimes the person can destroy your life without intending to do so. On the other hand, if the person is a supportive employer or someone like a mentor who is trying to increase your chances for success, then you probably would want to pay special attention to the person's ideas. The best way to tell whether the person is a friend is to put the person to the friend's litmus test. Ask yourself, "Is this person likely to lead me to danger or interfere with my success?"

One example is interfering with your schoolwork during class time by laughing and talking when the teacher is teaching. Think of each page of your textbook as a hundred dollar bill that you could earn when you graduate. Think of your textbook as a $25,000 down payment in gold bars on your $250,000 Lamborghini sports car. Letting a classmate steal opportunities for you to learn during class is like letting the person steal hundred dollar bills right out of your pocket.

Many times young men and women get into trouble because they don't take the time to figure out whether a person that they know is exposing them to something dangerous or encouraging them to do something that can be harmful. It is important to know how to perform a human litmus test to judge who is a friend and who is not.

**Explain in the space below how you will use the information you learned in this lesson to stay out of conflict and determine which of the people you spend time with are really your friends.**

_____

_____

_____

_____

_____

_____

_____

_____

_____

_____

_____

_____

_____

_____

_____

**Turning Girls into Ladies**

**A Multicultural, Behavioral Approach**

**Spirituality**

**Lesson 13**

**Turning Girls into Ladies**

**A Multicultural, Behavioral Approach**

**Spirituality**

**Lesson 13**

## Learning Objectives

You should learn:
- How to define two terms: "inner self" and "spirituality."
- How meditation helps you get in line with your inner self.
- To describe two ways in which the inner self is linked to the development of ladyhood.
- To experience quietness, stillness, and a peaceful state of mind during inner reflection exercises.
- How to monitor pleasurable bodily sensations during relaxation exercises.

**Exercise 13.1**
**Write your definition of spirituality in the section below.**

| Different Forms of Faith and a Continuum of Spiritual Belief | | | |
|---|---|---|---|
| **Level I** | **Level II** | **Level III** | **Level IV** |
| Faith in oneself based, belief in one's ability, personal experience, and values only. Atheist/Agnostic | Scientific faith based on numbers (data) and testing the world through experimentation Atheist/Agnostic | Combined scientific faith and faith in a higher power underlying the operation of the universe | Faith in a higher power based solely on belief (untested through experimentation and the collection of data) Belief in a higher power as the primary force affecting all things |
| Spiritual events probably do not exist | Physical measures and data are the gold standard for understanding the world and spiritual occurrences are irrelevant; based on numerical probability and repeated findings through ongoing experimentation | Physical measures and data are the gold standard for understanding the world with the assumption that the spiritual world picks up where science ends; based on numerical probability and repeated findings through ongoing experimentation | Spiritual occurrences are central to everything, and experimentation is unnecessary; Belief that world history and its current operation take place exactly as written in spiritual documents |
| Belief that what you detect through your five senses accurately represents the real world | Based on theory or a set of assumptions about ways that the universe operates | Based on theory or a set of assumptions about ways that the universe operates with a higher power as the driving force behind everything | Based on beliefs in undetectable forces in the universe based upon physical measurement |
| Little use of scientific data beyond personal experience | Belief that physical measurements from the world represent the real world accurately | Belief that physical measurements from the world represent the real world accurately and higher power forces are a relevant aspect of living in the world. | Physical measurement of occurrences in the world are not necessarily important compared to the influence of a higher power |

**Exercise 13.2**
**Where do your beliefs fit on the faith and spirituality chart? Explain why your beliefs fit at the level that you chose.**

_____

_____

_____

_____

_____

_____

_____

**Exercise 13.3**
**Spirituality**

The "inner self"

Spirituality is a way of getting in touch with the inner person who is deep inside of you. You may refer to this part of yourself as the "inner self." When a person gets in touch with her inner self, she recognizes her feelings and better trusts the feelings that are deep within herself.

Spirituality has always been an important part of belief systems in many communities. Spirituality is a way of life for many people of different ancestries. Spirituality is most meaningful through personal life experiences and community experiences.

Spirituality can provide a road map for living in a healthy, fulfilling way. Getting in touch with one's inner self can help you to be more in tune with the world. Having a good strong sense of your inner self helps a person to behave in ways that promote good health and wellbeing. Spirituality can lead to better relationships with others. It helps a young woman develop good character—the expression of close-to

109

universally accepted values and attitudes. The inner self also often guides many of the decisions that a mature person makes to embrace a positive future fully.

1. How would you describe your inner self?

2. How would you explain the meaning of spirituality or inner self to your friends and family?

3. What does becoming a lady have to do with spirituality?

4. What are some of the characteristics of someone who behaves in a "spiritual" manner?

5. What role has spirituality played in the history of different cultures around the world?

## SPIRITUALITY IS ROOTED IN THE HUMAN EXPERIENCE

Spirituality is the highest form of wisdom. Spirituality encompasses everything in life and provides a way of looking at life based on a young lady's life experiences. Through getting in touch with the inner self, which is an important part of spirituality, a young person develops a greater awareness of her inner self. Spirituality is rooted in the human experience, and it can lead to freedom from influences that keep young women from exercising good conscience, values, and decision-making skills.

**Exercise 13.3**
**Inner Self Stories**

**STEPS:** *What you do*
*Take 5 minutes to role-play the following scenarios.*

Scenario A
      A young woman and her friend were walking outside of the mall after shopping. She felt something in her coat pocket and asked what it was. The young woman told her friend that she stole an expensive bottle of cologne while they were in the store. The girl said she was going to tell her older brother who would scold her for stealing the cologne. The young woman pushed her away angrily, and shouted, "You are going to do what I say! You're not going to tell my brother anything about stealing this cologne."

Scenario B
      You were in a department store, and you noticed that someone had lost a wallet. In the wallet is $150.00 in cash and several credit cards. At first, you thought about taking the money and leaving the wallet and cards, but you decided to turn it into the customer service department. When you telephoned a friend to tell her you turned in the wallet, she called you stupid and said that you should have kept the money.

How could your spiritual beliefs affect the way that you respond in situations A and B?

What is the most mature way to handle each of these situations?

**Meditation Steps**

**Scientifically Tested Stress-Control Method**

1. Sit or lie in an exceptionally comfortable position.
2. Close your eyes.
3. Breathe air *very, very, very slowly* into your stomach through your nose so that your stomach looks full and fat.
4. *Hold your breath* for a safe and comfortable length of time.
5. *Breathe out very, very, very slowly* through your mouth.
6. *Hold your breath* again for a safe and comfortable length of time. Repeat steps 1-6.
7. At *exactly* the same time, *while breathing this way*, keep a calm image inside your head throughout the session. (Examples of calming mental scenes: Lying on the beach, floating in the clouds, enjoying nature in the forest on a sunny blue-sky day, walking through three to

four-foot, fresh-fallen snow the morning after a snowstorm. Note: It is normal to experience invasive thoughts. Practicing meditation helps to minimize nuisance thoughts.)

| MEDITATION<br>THE FACILITATOR WILL TAKE YOU THROUGH THE MEDITATION PROCESS. AFTERWARD, WRITE YOUR RESPONSES TO THE FOLLOWING QUESTIONS. |
| --- |
| • How easy or difficult was it to sit still and be quiet? |
| • What about your experience made it easy or difficult to tolerate quiet and stillness? |
| • How were you able to keep your mind from focusing on things other than the facilitator's instructions? |
| • What parts of the meditation exercise led to feelings of calm? |
| • How did you avoid any stress that the exercise may have caused? |
| • How relaxed did you feel in order to perform the reflective process? |
| • What aspects of the reflective process helped you to make the most out of the session? |
| • How can learning to be quiet and still help you to develop a greater sense of who you are as a young lady? |

# Turning Girls into Ladies

## A Multicultural, Behavioral Approach

## Fast Money vs. Honest Money

### Becoming a Success

### Lesson 14

**Turning Girls into Ladies**

**A Multicultural, Behavioral Approach**

**Fast Money vs. Honest Money**

**Becoming a Success**

**Lesson 14**

## Learning Objectives

You will learn about:

- Benefits and risks of pursuing a Fast Money vs. an Honest Money lifestyle.
- The relationship between hard work, quality, and success for a bright future.
- Actions that a person can take to become economically successful.

**Exercise 14.1**
**How to be SUCCESSFUL**

### Requirements for Success

Becoming successful in today's society is not always easy for any person. African American, Caucasian, Asian, Hispanic, and others have to overcome many of the same challenges to become successful in the world. Anyone in any of these groups can become successful through self-development and extremely hard work. Nothing worth having comes easy for many people. Attaining success in the 21st Century has always required preparation, dedication, self-sacrifice, and being willing to stick to a task until it is finished.

In this section, we will examine some of the skills and assets that females can use to earn a good income. Two paths that a person can take to achieve what she thinks is success is earning fast money or making honest money. Before we proceed, let's see what these terms can really mean.

### Definitions of Fast Money and Honest Money

Fast Money involves earning income, often more quickly than earning money honestly, by participating in socially unacceptable revenue-generating activities. Here are some examples of Fast Money activities:

- Selling illegal drugs on the street
- Stealing other people's work for financial gain
- Taking people's money by tricking them into making unprofitable investments

Honest Money involves earning income legally and by offering valuable goods and services and treating people fairly and truthfully. Examples of earning Honest Money are as follows:

- Running a plumbing business which is recognized for high-quality services by organizations like the Better Business Bureau
- Operating a restaurant that serves great tasting, nutritious food at a reasonable price
- Charging customers to make their lawns beautiful in a reasonable amount of time at an economical price

Often these ways of earning income yield large amounts of cash for a while, but some serious risks may be associated with Fast Money choices.

- What are the risks associated with earning fast money?
- What are the benefits associated with making honest money?

## Exercise 14.2
**Risks: FAST MONEY**

**STEPS: *What you do***
List 5 risks that accompany earning fast money.

1.

2.

3.

4.

5.

**Exercise 14.3**
**Benefits: HONEST MONEY**

**STEPS:** *What you do*
List 5 benefits that accompany earning honest money.

1.

2.

3.

4.

5.

**Exercise 14.4**

**Using Quality to BECOME SUCCESSFUL IN THE FUTURE**

People from all over the world come into contact with each other more frequently as the world appears to become smaller and more competitive. Frequently, young ladies who become the most successful are the ones who provide the best possible work, product, or service. Employers, business owners, and consumers demand higher and higher quality. Anyone who does not provide this quality will not be able to compete and earn a good living when compared to women who produce high-quality goods and services. Therefore, successful ladies need to completely embrace the following statement to thrive in the 21st Century and beyond:

*Quality is the single most important item that distinguishes successful from unsuccessful ladies in the future. The way to success is by engaging in good, long-term planning. That means planning many months or perhaps years ahead. Producing high quality means providing goods and services that meet or exceed standards of excellence. Most industries have standards or benchmarks that tell producers and consumers what products and services are the best. The most competitive business ladies provide high-quality services and sell the best products. They maintain close, warm relationships with customers so that customers feel good about coming back to the competitive lady for additional goods and services. When used over the long term, this approach can make a woman rich and successful. It can also be rewarding and make her feel good about the work that she performs.*

Your job is to find out what you have to do to produce the highest level of quality for every project that you complete. This is true, no matter what your field of work is. Many jobs have differing but high sets of expectations that you have to meet for people to consider your work to be of high quality. What you need to do to be successful in the next several decades and beyond is to develop a reputation for providing high-quality goods and services. If you do this, many people will want to come back to you over and over before they consider going to anyone else for your goods and services.

In this way, a successful lady gets paid multiple times for a string of great products and services instead of getting paid only once for inferior work. People do not want to do repeated business with women who perform substandard work. The starting place for training yourself to appreciate and produce high-quality work is in middle school and continues into high school. It goes on this way through college, or a noncollege route if you choose that direction, and through your adult experiences on the job. What you do in family, school, community, and in your work life to perfect the quality of your work will all lead to building an important foundation for success in the future.

| Risks and Benefits of Different Ways of Earning a Living | |
|---|---|
| Fast Money Risks | Honest Money Benefits (such as, respectable employment or owning your own business) |
| Likelihood of long-term jail sentence | Safety of associating with law-abiding people |
| Jail time leading to exposure to physical, mental, and sexual abuse | Peace of mind from earning an honorable living |
| Limited job, contract, teamwork opportunities with honest people | Creative freedom |
| Poor health choices such as contracting sexual diseases because of corrupt peer influences | A good insurance in case of a health emergency and the ability to choose your own doctors |
| Reduced lifetime earning potential | Set your own financial earnings method and goals—no earning limits |
| Becoming a victim of violence—by being double-crossed, criminal conspiracy, etc. (No honor among thieves and other criminals) | The choice to live in a safe, protected environment |
| Damaged reputation | Freedom to pursue your dreams and passions |

**Exercise 14.5**
**Two Earnings Approaches: Fast Money vs. Honest Money**

Compare the Fast Money and Honest Money charts. What are your thoughts about which of the two charts is the better choice. Explain in detail why you think one chart is better than the other one. Write your responses below.

_____

_____

_____

_____

**Fast Money vs. Honest Money Income Patterns**

What do you notice about this person's income level before and after prison on the Fast Money Income chart? Write your comments.

_____

_____

_____

What do you notice about the pattern of increase in income level on the Honest Money Income chart? Write your comments.

_____

_____

_____

How does the amount of lifetime earnings on the fast money chart compare with earnings on the honest money chart?

_____

_____

_____

How many times more money does the honest person make compared to the dishonest person?

_____

_____

_____

How do the average annual average income and the average hourly earnings compare with each other for the Fast Money versus Honest Money Income charts?

_____

_____

_____

What are your conclusions about using the fast money versus the honest money approach to becoming successful?

_____

_____

_____

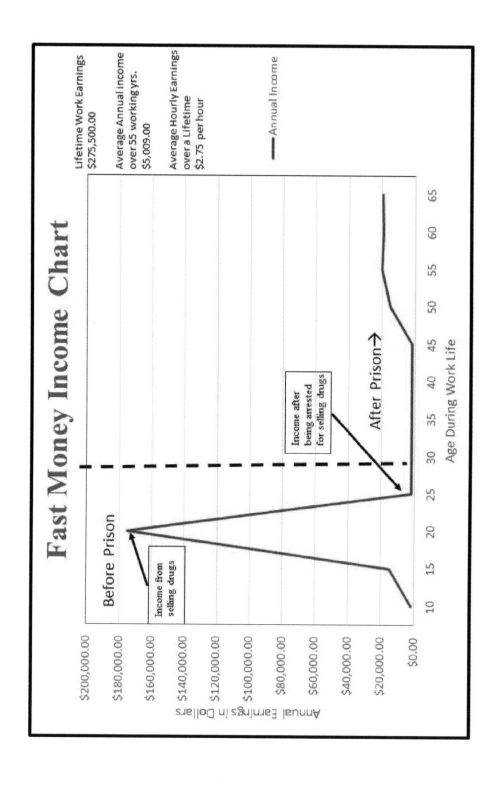

Fast Money Income Chart

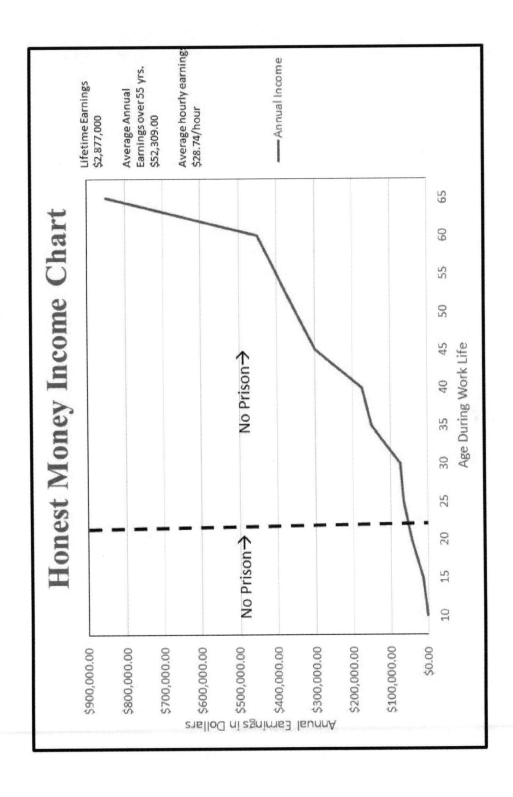

Honest Money Income Chart

Lifetime Earnings $2,877,000

Average Annual Earnings over 55 yrs. $52,309.00

Average hourly earnings $28.74/hour

—— Annual Income

No Prison→

No Prison→

Annual Earnings in Dollars
$900,000.00
$800,000.00
$700,000.00
$600,000.00
$500,000.00
$400,000.00
$300,000.00
$200,000.00
$100,000.00
$0.00

Age During Work Life
10  15  20  25  30  35  40  45  50  55  60  65

121

**Exercise 14.6**
**Characteristics of the Successful Lady**
The young person:

- Is honest with herself about her shortcomings and understands that there is always going to be someone who knows more or can do something better than her.
- Rather than being envious or holding onto ill feelings toward others, she uses others' abilities as a source of encouragement and motivation to do better herself.
- Takes personal responsibility for overcoming hardships and doesn't waste time and energy blaming other people for her current situation if the situation is difficult.
- Avoids waiting for others to tell her what to do to be successful. She reviews her own goals and behavior and makes frequent, appropriate changes that are necessary to achieve these goals.
- Checks the quality of her work without being told.
- Corrects errors and strives to produce the very best work product available.
- Is realistic about what she can achieve one step at a time and recognizes that large earnings usually come from a gradual movement from one stepping stone to another.

**Managing Money: Budgeting**
**How to Keep Your Money**

One of the most important actions that a young lady can take after achieving financial stability is to learn ways to manage her money. This is another mark of a leader. She learns how to exercise self-control to use her funds in a way that allows her to maintain a comfortable lifestyle while investing in her future.

*MAINTAINING A COMFORTABLE LONG-TERM WAY OF LIFE USUALLY INVOLVES LEARNING TO SPEND FAR LESS THAN YOUR DISPOSABLE LEVEL OF INCOME!*

The next step is to plan a successful way to pay important bills EXACTLY ON TIME and, at the same time, save enough money to prepare for the future. In order to create a good plan for managing her money, the *WISE* young lady must outline all of her expenses versus sources of income. The successful young lady's responsibility as a mature leader is to lay out all of the categories of spending and income that she will experience every week, two weeks, or every month. The example listed here is monthly.

A young lady needs to stick with the listed items presented in all of her spending areas. The way for her to stick with an intelligent plan for spending is called budgeting. Making a budget is not difficult as long as you identify realistic costs for each expense that you list on the budget and to never spend more than you make.

The other key point that she must take into account is to make sure that she includes every major cost that applies to her. Examples may include house payment or rent, food, clothing, electric bill, natural gas bill, car payment, telephone, cable or satellite, car insurance, clothing, department store, school, and personal loans. It is also important to consider work hours and pay when putting together a budget strategy. Other areas include costs like money for starting a family, going to a trade school, or starting a business. These expenditures call for saving money for investment in the future.

Some ways to become successful legally are by putting in extra work hours on a job, creating and perfecting smart business approaches and plans, and saving money to achieve life goals. It makes sense to develop or revise a success plan every year. Write down your goals and objectives and include realistic deadlines for completing each goal or objective. (Note: Goals are general areas that you want to improve. Objectives are measurable projected changes in your performance that anyone else can verify by checking out your initial intentions against final achievements.)

| KEYS TO MANAGING MY SUCCESS |
| THINK ABOUT WHAT THE WORDS OR PHRASES BELOW MEAN TO YOU PERSONALLY. |

| | |
| --- | --- |
| 1 | Self-sacrifice |
| 2 | Self-discipline |
| 3 | Independent thinking |
| 4 | Planning |
| 5 | Working a plan |
| 6 | Monitoring your progress |
| 7 | Seeking out wise people with whom to associate |
| 8 | Withstanding rejection from people who say that they are your friends |

Describe various ways in which you will use these terms to achieve success in your life.

_____

_____

_____

Considering the terms just mentioned for managing your life, in what ways do you see your future "SUCCESS" as being financially driven versus your success being dependent on your personal goals?

_____

_____

_____

**Exercise 14.7**
**Keeping Control Over Your Money**

**STEPS:** *What you do*
*Now let's learn how to keep control of your money by preparing a budget.*

Now complete the budget on the next page, and then return to the bottom of this page to answer the three questions. Start by writing the monthly income at the top of the chart (For example, $5,000 per month). Fill in each of the items or bills (that is, Giving, Savings, House/Rent, Utilities, etc.) going down the budget chart page for the following headings:

**ITEM OR BILLS, Monthly Total, Payoff Total, How Far Behind**

Notice that the headings go from left to right at the top of the chart. Now add the total at the bottom of the page for each of these headings. Answer the following questions.

How much money would you have at the end of the month if you paid all of the bills that you listed in your Monthly Totals?

How much money would you need to pay off the total for each of these bills? Write in a proposed dollar figure for the total amount of money that you have saved.

Write several sentences to describe how far behind or ahead you would be in meeting the requirements of your monthly budget.

_____

_____

_____

## Managing Money with a Basic Budget

Monthly income: _____

| Items or Bills | Monthly Total | Payoff Total | How Far Behind |
|---|---|---|---|
| Giving | | | |
| Savings | | | |
| House/Rent | | | |
| Utilities | | | |
| Electricity | _____ | _____ | _____ |
| Water | _____ | _____ | _____ |
| Natural Gas | _____ | _____ | _____ |
| Phone | _____ | _____ | _____ |
| Trash Collection | _____ | _____ | _____ |
| Cable/Internet | _____ | _____ | _____ |
| Food | _____ | _____ | _____ |
| Transportation | _____ | _____ | _____ |
| Car Payment | _____ | _____ | _____ |
| Gas & Oil | _____ | _____ | _____ |
| Repair & Tires | _____ | _____ | _____ |
| Car Insurance | _____ | _____ | _____ |
| Clothing | _____ | _____ | _____ |
| Personal | _____ | _____ | _____ |
| Health Insurance | _____ | _____ | _____ |
| Child Care | _____ | _____ | _____ |
| Entertainment | _____ | _____ | _____ |
| Other Miscellaneous | _____ | _____ | _____ |
| Totals | _____ | _____ | _____ |

**Turning Girls into Ladies**

**A Multicultural, Behavioral Approach**

**Becoming a Mature, Well-Rounded Lady**

**Lesson 15**

**Turning Girls into Ladies**

**A Multicultural, Behavioral Approach**

**Becoming a Mature, Well-Rounded Lady**

**Lesson 15**

## Objectives

You will learn about:
- What it means to become a thoroughly mature, overall lady leader.
- Ways to avoid being a little girl in a woman's bodies—maximizing maturity.
- Five ways to develop yourself into a complete lady from youth to old age.
- Ways to become a better woman and leader by working to improve your community.

This program, Turning Girls into Ladies, started out by reviewing the differences between actions that girls take compared to behaviors that mature ladies perform. Just because a female is older does not necessarily mean that she is a mature or well-rounded woman. Too many female and male adults are fully grown in years but lack the social maturity that makes them a well-rounded person. Fortunately, because of this program, you will better understand what it means to be a more well-rounded, mature lady. You will have opportunities to practice skills and discuss concepts that will help you to achieve greater social maturity and to become a more well-balanced, successful lady.

**Exercise 15.1**
**Maturity Characteristics**

Examine the chart on the next page to see the difference between immature girls and mature ladies. Before you do that, let's look at a definition of social maturity so that it is clearer exactly what the point of this section of the lesson is about.

Social maturity is a well-developed ability to behave effectively according to social rules and standards. These rules fit each person's age as measured in years. Social maturity involves making healthy, productive choices in response to people and situations which a female or male encounters throughout each stage of life.

## The Socially and Emotionally Mature Lady

| A Baby Girl inside of a Grown Woman's Body | A Healthy Well-Balance Grown Woman |
|---|---|
| Too many adult females (and adult males) act like young children on the inside.<br><br>Some women who behave this way can have a personality problem called being narcissistic, according to mental health therapists. Just like a little kid, they behave as follows:<br>Unable to put themselves in other people's shoes and see situations the way other people do.<br>Fail to follow through on their promises. Can do no wrong in their words - everyone else is wrong.<br>Always want to be in the limelight.<br>Ashamed of themselves deep down inside.<br>Dislike themselves deep inside.<br>Project a false or perfect image of themselves to other people.<br>Refuse to accept responsibility for their faults.<br>Pretend that other people always hurt them—"victim complex."<br>Take credit for work they did not do.<br>Unlikely to help people unless they know they get something out of it.<br>Prone to temper tantrums or sulking when they don't get their way.<br>Get quiet or mad when someone disagrees or criticizes them.<br>Envious of others and think others are envious of them.<br>Little or no compassion or feelings for others; emotionally dead.<br>Crave praise and attention.<br>Treat other people like things to be used and thrown away.<br>Little or no sense of right or wrong.<br>See people or situations in black or white, all or none.<br>Tell little and big lies whenever it suits their purpose.<br>Unpredictably mean and irritable.<br>Like to ignore or give people the cold shoulder.<br>Manipulative, critical, and judgmental of others.<br>(They can dish out criticism, but they cannot take it.)<br>Pretend to care and love but don't really care about or love people.<br>Prefer one-way relationships only, if possible, extremely controlling and have many rules for others to follow which they feel no need to follow themselves.<br><br>"A small, child-like woman" | Some women can be 60 years old but act like children on the inside. The emotionally grown-up lady behaves as follows:<br><br>Other people's feelings, quality of life, and dreams are just as important as those of the mature lady.<br>Capable of caring and love in intimate relationships with other people.<br>Hostility and possessiveness have no place in her relationships with others.<br>Self-love, self-acceptance, and emotional security allow her to handle frustrating situations without overreacting to small sources of irritation. Easily able to exercise self-control, waits long periods for rewards, and adjusts relatively effortlessly to situations beyond her control.<br>Good reasoning and judgment that is unaffected by emotional distortions of the truth. Able to accept valid feedback from well-meaning, competent individuals.<br>Understands herself in a way that suggests that she has accurate and meaningful self-insight.<br>Able to laugh at herself and use humor in a way that builds relationships with other people.<br>Believes in a universal view of the world such as belief in a higher power, God, the connection among universal systems.<br>Reaches out to people rather than waiting for people to reach out to her.<br>Extends a warm, accepting, and tolerant way of dealing with people.<br>Active, effective, and strong values, which she actually follows for the most part.<br><br>"A Grand, Mature, Lady"<br><br>Gordon Allport as cited in Hall, C. S., in Lindzey, G. Theories of personality. New York: John Wiley & Sons, Inc. 1970. |

| The Difference between Girls and Socially Mature Ladies | | | | | |
|---|---|---|---|---|---|
| Choose which column matches the behavior of girls versus mature ladies. Select one answer for each item. | | | | | |
| Items | Girls | Ladies | | Girls | Ladies |
| 1. Takes responsibility for her actions | | | 18. Is self-centered | | |
| 2. Considers other people's feelings routinely | | | 19. Easily influenced by peers | | |
| 3. Promotes nonviolence with people who live around her | | | 20. Ruins people and places around her | | |
| 4. Gets drunk or high when she feels like it | | | 21. Puts others down regularly | | |
| 5. Earns items that she uses personally | | | 22. Reacts to negative events rather than avoiding them beforehand | | |
| 6. Respects people by protecting them | | | 23. Physically mistreats others | | |
| 7. Respects property by protecting it | | | 24. Emotionally mistreats others | | |
| 8. Obeys the law | | | 25. Thinks of herself more often than others | | |
| 9. Promotes people's healthy thoughts and actions among people | | | 26. Praises herself more often than others | | |
| 10. Shows self-control | | | 27. Accepts harmful ideas without considering their effects on others | | |
| 11. Maintains self-discipline | | | 28. Starts verbal or physical fights | | |

| | | | | | | |
|---|---|---|---|---|---|---|
| 12. Makes people around her feel stronger | | | 29. Uses belongings of others without permission | | | |
| 13. Shows patience | | | 30. Takes advantage of others' belongings | | | |
| 14. Completes tasks without quitting | | | 31. Shares little of her time or talent with the community | | | |
| 15. Tolerates others | | | 32. Insists that self-restraint is pointless | | | |
| 16. Gives back to the community | | | 33. Jumps from one project to another prematurely | | | |
| 17. Avoids toxic substances like alcohol and drugs | | | 34. Meets project deadlines routinely | | | |

**The Lady's Journey**

Becoming a lady who is a well-developed, balanced, successful, and mature leader is an uphill climb, but it is an achievable goal. It is also a never-ending process because it is always important to strive for bettering yourself.

Increasingly, successful female leaders from every racial, ethnic, educational, and social background are discovering that they can never become satisfied with just getting by. Successful leaders recognize that they must always be looking for ways to improve or reinvent themselves. Anyone who fails to engage in a continuous improvement process will become outdated in the job market and the business arena.

One reason why ladies must become comfortable with change has to do with the ongoing developments in the uses of computers and other applications of science. Computers, telecommunications, and the Internet have all put a different face on the lifestyle of every person in the "developed" world. More importantly, major cities and suburban communities encounter new issues because of constant shifts in ethnic and racial living patterns. To adjust to frequent changes, because of technology and social environments, everyone has to look for opportunities to make dramatic improvements in their value to society and for their own advancement.

Smart female leaders of the future will be looking for ways to get an edge over the competition. The way to advance beyond the competition is to become a better you. That often results in putting money in your pocket. This can involve taking refresher courses in different subject areas. It can require changing fields of work completely when necessary. For example, the lady who worked as a cashier for 15 years goes back to school to learn computerized shipping of supply orders online. In another case, the young lady who worked in a fast-food restaurant returns to school to learn a skilled trade like becoming a chef, caterer, or event coordinator. A young lady who has repaired computers for five years may desire to start her own business that specializes in making computer upgrades. These women increase their success in part because of their willingness to keep in touch with changes in the job market.

Another asset is each young lady's ability to roll with the punches. Rather than complain about having few opportunities, these female leaders create their own opportunities. They learn new skills, keep up with new opportunities, and take advantage of these opportunities.

Keeping in touch with career opportunities and responding to them is an important matter for a young aspiring lady to think about. Yet, earning a comfortable living is not the only area that a young woman needs to take into account. Let's take a look at some of the ways in which a young lady can move beyond simply earning a living to becoming a well-rounded, polished, and sophisticated individual.

**Exercise 15.2**
**Self-Inventory**

<table>
<tr><td colspan="6">THE YOUNG LADY'S DEVELOPMENT<br>CLASS THROUGH EXPOSURE TO MANY<br>ELEMENTS OF LIFE<br>LADYHOOD DEVELOPMENT</td></tr>
<tr><td colspan="6">First, examine the following pie chart. Then come back to this page and check the box to the right that best describes your choice for each one of the behaviors described below. Choose one box for each item that best describes the way that you act.</td></tr>
<tr><td>Items</td><td>Not at all like me</td><td>Slightly like me</td><td>Somewhat like me</td><td>Like me</td><td>Exactly like me</td></tr>
<tr><td>1. I am a person who educates myself by participating in activities like reading, taking formal classes, and volunteering to help others.</td><td></td><td></td><td></td><td></td><td></td></tr>
<tr><td>2. I am a person who travels away from home (national or international).</td><td></td><td></td><td></td><td></td><td></td></tr>
<tr><td>3. I am a person who mingles with people from different backgrounds, education, and cultures.</td><td></td><td></td><td></td><td></td><td></td></tr>
<tr><td>4. I am a person who pursues wisdom from seasoned and experienced people (wise counsel).</td><td></td><td></td><td></td><td></td><td></td></tr>
<tr><td>5. I am a person who attends artistic, cultural, and educational events.</td><td></td><td></td><td></td><td></td><td></td></tr>
</table>

# LADYHOOD DEVELOPMENT
## CULTIVATING CLASS THROUGH
## EXPOSURE TO ENRICHING ELEMENTS OF LIFE

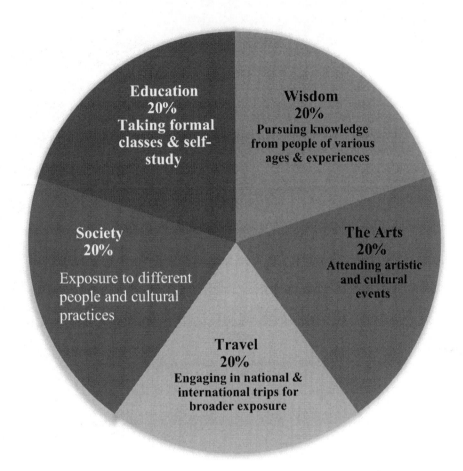

**Exercise 15.3 Restructuring Your Thoughts**

> **Describe your reasons for rating each of the previous _five_ items the way that you did. Why did you avoid describing the item as being "Not at all like" you, what would have caused you to make the choice that the item was "Exactly like" you?**

**Write your answers below.**

_____

_____

_____

_____

_____

**Janet Success**
**Ways to Think about Beating Your Competition**

Here is another way to achieve high standards of success in your life. Imagine that you are in a race for life against one of the best competitors that you will ever meet. This ideal competitor is another version of you, and this ideal version of yourself is named "Janet Success." (Both you and Janet have identical race cars, and the goal is to drive the superhighway of life to the top of Challenge Mountain and over the top of the mountain into Success Valley.

"Janet Success"

This is what you have to think about. Janet Success is a winner because she is a fierce competitor. In other words, she is always looking for ways to get an advantage over you in this race. Thus, Janet is bent on doing anything and everything that she can legally do to win the race against you. Janet is looking for ways to improve herself, her car, the way that she drives her car, or anything else that she can do to insure that she is going to beat you in the race. That means dressing in the latest race course uniform, tuning up her car, using the best gasoline, oil, tires, transmission fluid, brakes, and so on possible to win the race against you.

She is fired up about winning at all times. She goes to sleep thinking about winning the race and then wakes up thinking about ways to beat you. She thinks about what lane to drive in to be able to pass you on the road of life. How fast does she need to drive in light of the distance of the life course so that she does not run out of gas? She is determined to beat you across the finish line.

Now, remember that there are many Janet Successes in the world who are always investing in themselves at all times to be the best race car driver that they can be. While Janet is speeding down the race course at over 150 miles per hour, too many young women (and young men) are sitting on the side of the road in the park or creeping along the highway in low gear at 30 miles per hour. Instead of asking themselves what they can do to improve their vehicle of a lifetime, they point fingers at the other drivers. The most successful women strive to get their lives in order by watching Janet Success and doing whatever they need to do to win. In this way, they are able to place themselves in a position to be able to compete in the race of life. The question is, are you placing yourself in a competitive position with Janet Success, or are you sitting on the side of the road in the park?

What actions do you need to take in your life to make yourself competitive with Janet Success?

_____

_____

_____

_____

_____

_____

Janet Success learns the rules of the race better than any of the other drivers so that she knows how to drive her vehicle straight into Success Valley. That includes looking the part of a winning race car driver and outstanding competitor. Looking and acting the part of a winner is *called impression management*. How do you need to change your appearance in a way that maximizes your competitiveness in the race of life? What about your means of managing the way you come across to people who could help you to outperform Janet?

_____

_____

_____

_____

A friend will never lead you to danger or interfere with your success. How would Janet insure that she has people in her life who help her to insure that she wins the race to Success Valley?

_____

_____

_____

_____

**Exercise 15.4**

**Impression Management: Ways to Maximize Your Marketability and Competitiveness in the Business and Work World.**

**THE WAY THAT YOU "CARRY" YOURSELF ADDS TO YOUR BOTTOM LINE!**

**DEFINE THE TERMS BELOW USING YOUR OWN WORDS.**

1.  Class—Professional Look

2.  Dignity—Noble character, manner, or language; worthy of respect

3.  Style—Individual expression of taste in actions and choices

**Explain how managing the way that you present yourself to people (impression management) in business and at work can increase the amount of money that you make.**

_____

_____

_____

### Exercise 15.5 Acquiring Social Polish
### Cell Phone Impression Management

**Manners that Pay Off with Dollars and Respect**

A very important area that has to be an enormous concern for young ladies who want to succeed is cell phone use in public, social etiquette and manners. Remember that the use of cell phones in public places like restaurants, movie theaters, professional offices, and so on is considered ill-mannered and undignified. Carrying on a public conversation about private business is considered rude, crude, uncivilized, and unintelligent. You will need to avoid using cellular telephones in these locations unless it is an absolute emergency. If it is an emergency, leave the area and go to a private location where no one can easily hear your conversation.

Always represent yourself in a polished and sophisticated manner. You never know when the next employer, talent scout, or potential business partner is watching. It would be unfortunate to lose money by missing out on your next opportunity because of a lack of social polish in your life. Imagine if someone saw you as being so lacking in manners and home training that they did not want to work with you.

Also, recognize that the way you carry yourself reflects on the reputation of your family as a whole. Conduct yourself in the most dignified and sophisticated manner possible without being judgmental, artificial, or snobbish. Using cellular telephones in private locations for routine conversations is a sign of intelligence and being well-raised. It makes your parents and family look like they did a good job of preparing you to operate in society. It also helps you to be more competitive in job and business settings and can contribute to building your finances.

**What are your thoughts about using a cell phone in a restaurant to talk loudly to friends and associates when the topic is not an emergency? What if you are disturbing the other customers? How can this affect the way important people respect you or avoid working with you? Write out your responses below.**

_____

_____

_____

_____

_____

_____

**Exercise 15.6 Manners Matter**
**SHOWING SOCIAL MANNERS**
**Consider how the following behaviors could favorably affect your relationships with others. What is your responsibility for insuring that you are practicing good manners consistently?**

- Keep your mouth closed while chewing
- No singing while eating food
- One hand in your lap at the dinner table
- Elbows off the table at a dinner event
- Place your napkin in lap
- Always being courteous and considerate toward others
- Opening doors for others, especially ladies
- Never interrupting conversations or by talking while others are talking
- Keeping offensive or hurtful comments to yourself regardless of whether they are true

Saying, "Yes, Sir. No, Sir. Yes, Ma'am. No, Ma'am," to older adults.

**Exercise 15.7 Becoming Your Personal Best**
**Which of these behaviors could you work on to become more polished and sophisticated?**
**Write out your explanation in detail below.**

_____

_____

_____

_____

_____

_____

**Exercise 15.8 Becoming a Respectful Real Lady**
**Think about the working definition of a respectful real lady. Write a paragraph about how you can become a real woman who shows respect to other people with acceptable social conduct.**

Working definition:

A real woman: Demonstrates respect for herself, males, peers, family, adults, and community.

_____

_____

_____

_____

_____

_____

_____

_____

_____

_____

| Exercise 15.9 Thinking Independently | | |
|---|---|---|
| YOU DECIDE | | |
| LOOK AT THE WORDS BELOW. BASED ON WHAT YOU LEARNED IN THIS TRAINING, CHECK EITHER GIRLHOOD OR LADYHOOD FOR WHERE YOU BELIEVE YOU ARE RIGHT NOW. (BE HONEST.) | Girlhood | Ladyhood |
| 1. Profanity | | |
| 2. Independence | | |
| 3. Tolerance | | |
| 4. Resistance to change | | |
| 5. Selfishness | | |
| 6. Consideration towards others | | |
| 7. Anticipation of the needs of others | | |

**Exercise 15.10 Ladyhood Lessons Learned: A Review**

**More considerations of what it takes to be a mature lady.**
**Thinking back over the information that you have reviewed in this program, what do you consider to be the most important for helping you to grow and mature into a well-rounded lady? Write out your thoughts in summary below.**

- Avoids cursing—especially in public. Not only does cursing in public make you look immature, but it also makes you look foolish and uncultured.
- Thinks for herself to do what she knows is right.
- Tolerance for rejection from friends and acquaintances. Remember: *A friend will never lead you to danger or interfere with your success.* You can always make new friends who will meet this definition of a real friend.
- Learns to make wise decisions about what information is good for her mental health. Manages her responsibilities, bills, motherhood, work, and education.
- Treats others with respect and consideration. Acts as a protector and not a perpetrator!
- A mature leader learns to balance all of these areas for the good of her intimate partner, family, and community. A mature leader spends some of her time putting the community first. She is noble in this regard.
- A mature leader imagines herself in others' shoes often and demonstrates compassion toward others. When necessary, she stands up for others in an appropriate way.
- Unless a young lady deliberately cultivates these qualities in herself consistently in her life, she cannot be truly successful as a well-integrated and balanced person.

_____

_____

_____

_____

_____

**Exercise 15.11 Negotiating Government and Political Systems: Exercising the Power of a Lady**

Learning how to negotiate systems like government, education, medical, and political systems is an important way to improve the quality of life for all people. The more you learn in this area, the better you will be able to improve your life and those around you. Learn how systems work legally and honestly. Take the time to find out how agencies and organizations work where people who make decisions do so successfully. Use their methods to influence politics and decision making when the agencies' methods are respectable and legal. Find out who the decision-makers are and learn ways to influence their decision-making. You have more power and influence than you recognize.

1.  How would you describe the quality of your skills and abilities in this area?

2.  What actions do you need to take to become proficient in each of these areas?

3.  Describe your aspirations in each of these areas?

**Exercise 15.12 Becoming a Lady as an Effective Agent of Change**

Learn to access government systems, community agencies, corporations, etc. at points in the organization where you can make a difference in the way the community runs. If you do not gain satisfaction with the first person that you contact in an organization, continue making contacts until you find a sympathetic decision-maker. Look inside an organization and outside at agencies who work directly with the one you are interested in changing. Learn how to change laws and policies that affect your life and the lives of other people favorably. Most importantly, if you feel really strongly about what you are doing, do not give up under any circumstances.

1.  How would you describe the quality of your skills and abilities in this area?

2.  What actions do you need to take to become proficient in each of these areas?

3.  Describe your aspirations in each of these areas?

**Exercise 15.13 Networking and Resiliency Networking**

Meet influential and seemingly non-influential people and form positive, genuine working relationships with all of them. Never underestimate the value of anyone! Treat everyone with respect at all times! Healthy relationships with other people make the world function seamlessly! Try to find common ground with other people who may have the same interests that you do. Branch out from these individuals to others who have interests similar to yours. The truly mature lady multiplies her effectiveness by strengthening relationships with others. Her goal is always to form positive, honest, trustworthy, and genuine relationships with others.

1.  How would you describe the quality of your skills and abilities in this area?

2.  What actions do you need to take to become proficient in each of these areas?

3.  Describe your aspirations in each of these areas?

## Closing Thoughts: Becoming the Perfect Lady

Remember that it would be rare, if not impossible, for any one person to display _ALL_ of the qualities outlined in the lessons presented here for leaders like you to COMPLETELY develop their role as a perfect lady with absolute maturity. Why expect that? This is a lifelong growth and learning process with forward and backward movements along the way. No one expects a lady to be perfect—just always moving toward perfection! The main point is that you exhibit an overall forward movement in the direction that this program is taking your behavior.
HERE ARE SOME IMPORTANT PARTING WORDS:
The key qualities of the ideal lady that you should consider pursuing as a fully developed leader include cultivating in yourself:

Maturity
Responsibility
Sisterhood
Good physical development—nutrition & exercise
Strong mental health
Following laws and worldwide standards
Honest achievement
Pursuit of high quality in all things
Respect, especially for others
Genuine concern for others—reaching back and reaching out a violence-free
lifestyle
A body free from contaminating substances like illicit drugs
Ongoing movement towards becoming a polished, well-mannered lady of sophistication.

The growth process never ends. The important point is that you do not necessarily have to display ALL of these qualities immediately or all at once. The journey toward becoming a mature, well-rounded lady is as important as the destination or goal.
A mature, whole lady will always work to pursue these virtues as a leader who constantly redefines herself for the changing needs in her circumstances and the world. Yet she remains an independent thinker. In this way, you, and young ladies like you, will be better prepared to face the challenges of the ideal lady in the years 2050, 2150, 2250, and beyond. Also, learn to give yourself credit where credit is due for the progress that you make in these areas. If you follow the recommendations listed in this program, you will be in a much better position to excel in life.

Best wishes, and thank you for caring about yourself and your future.

**YOU DESERVE SUCCESS!**

Selected sources for key research-based behavioral principles used in the program

## Behavior Modification and Cognitive-Behavioral Reading List

Behavior Modification Principles and Procedures, Fifth Edition, Raymond G. Miltenberger, Cengage Learning, 2016.

International Handbook of Behavior Modification and Therapy, Alan S. Bellack, Plenum Press, 1982.

Behavior Modification: What It Is and How To Do It, Tenth Edition 10th Edition, Garry Martin & Joseph J. Pear, Routledge, 2016.

Behavior Principles in Everyday Life (4th Edition) 4th Edition, John D. Baldwin & Janice I. Baldwin, Delmar Cengage Learning, 2010.

Applied Behavior Analysis (2nd Edition), John O. Cooper, Timothy E. Heron, and William L. Heward, Pearson Education Limited, 2013.

Made in the USA
Columbia, SC
14 June 2023